Praise for *Organizing Genius*

"The most riveting management book ever, *Organizing Genius* has the swashbuckling stories of seven 'Great Groups' who changed the world and how they were led. . . . These are genuinely classic cases of what Brian Eno calls 'scenius'—group genius. Besides retelling the stories well, Warren Bennis has the insight (he's the author of excellent books on leadership) to tease out the elements that Great Groups have in common."

Global Business Network book club newsletter

"Warren Bennis's latest book, and one of his best, teases out organizing secrets [to] show through case studies that great groups are project-driven. . . . The authors 'deliver' abundant clues on why some people just work together, and others collaborate for extraordinary achievement."

Cincinnati Enquirer

"Mention the name Warren Bennis and the word 'leadership' springs to mind. This latest book by Bennis and coauthor Patricia Ward Biederman . . . has to rank among his most interesting, entertaining and, ultimately, practical contributions. The stories are insightful, the lessons are well-formulated. For every manager who is confronted with the question, How can I get my people to do a better job? this book provides useful ideas."

Organizational Dynamics

"Working from the assumption that 'none of us is as smart as all of us,'. . . *Organizing Genius* attempts to uncover the elements of creative collaboration by examining six of this century's most extraordinary groups. . . . The stories of how these groups broke new ground make for engrossing reading."

The President

"Any new book by Warren Bennis is an event to get excited about. . . . In *Organizing Genius* Bennis and Biederman examine six Great Groups in such diverse areas as politics, animation, and the arts. . . . These are the lessons that virtually any organization can learn and commit to in order to transform its own management team into a collaborative and successful group of leaders."

Government Training News

"This well-written book contains an amazing summary (within a relatively small space of 229 pages) of the workings of highly gifted groups. The story of these groups can help educators of the gifted to organize authentic and dynamic cooperative learning environments in their schools and classrooms."

Gifted Education News-Page

"*Organizing Genius* is long overdue—a jargon-free, pleasure-to-read study of a special kind of teamwork, the kind that sets out to do the impossible and does."

Alvin and Heidi Toffler, authors of *The Third Wave*

"Creative collaboration is the élan vitale of all organizations striving for excellence, and the Take-Home Lessons provided by Professor Bennis and Ms. Biederman will equally benefit the League of Women Voters and Southwest Airlines."

Herb Kelleher, Chairman, President, and CEO, Southwest Airlines

"*Organizing Genius* is another inspiring, timely contribution from the thought leader of leadership studies, Warren Bennis. It illuminates with wisdom and stories one of the most essential issues for 21st-century managers: how to create 'collaborative advantage' by turning individual talent into teamwork."

Rosabeth Moss Kanter, author of *World Class*

ORGANIZING

---

*"None of us
is as smart
as all of us."*

GENIUS

The Secrets of Creative Collaboration

Warren Bennis

Patricia Ward Biederman

BASIC
BOOKS

A Member of the Perseus Books Group
New York

Many of the designations used by manufacturers and sellers to distinguish their products are claimed as trademarks. Where those designations appear in this book and Perseus Books was aware of a trademark claim, the designations have been printed in initial capital letters (e.g., Macintosh).

Library of Congress Cataloging-in-Publication Data

Bennis, Warren G.
Organizing genius : the secret of creative collaboration / Warren Bennis, Patricia Ward Biederman.
     p.   cm.
"None of us is as smart as all of us."
Includes bibliographical references and index.

ISBN 0-201-57051-3 (hardcover)
ISBN 10: 0-201-33989-7 (paperback)
ISBN 13: 978-0-201-33989-5 (paperback)

1. Organizational effectiveness—Case studies.   2. Strategic alliances (Business)—Case studies.   3. Creative thinking—Case studies.   4. Creative ability in business—Case studies.
I. Biederman, Patricia Ward.   II. Title.
HD58.9.B45   1997
158.7—dc20   96-41454
                                                       CIP

Previously published by Perseus Publishing
Basic Books is a member of the Perseus Books Group
Cover design by Suzanne Heiser
Text design by Wilson Graphics
Set in 13-point Bembo by Shepard Poorman

30   29   28   27   26   25   24   23   22   21

To my darling Grace,
who has watched over every word of this book
as lovingly as she has watched over me

Warren Bennis

To Rosalie Marie Ward
and Eric Paul Biederman,
who made all things possible

Patricia Ward Biederman

CONTENTS

FOREWORD

There are groups, and there are Great Groups. To turn the first into the second must be every leader's dream. This book provides the clues, provokes some questions, and leaves some mystery remaining.

Great Groups hope to "make a dent in the universe," as Steve Jobs told the team that created the Macintosh computer. They flare like a rocket for a while, then vanish, leaving behind their creation, be it the first atom bomb, a new kind of college, an amazing computer, or a family of cartoon characters to delight the world. Can they ever repeat the trick, one wonders, or are they like butterflies given one brief but beautiful life? And is there life after the group for its members, or must they settle for a form of immortality, one given them by their creation?

Warren Bennis's great gift is the ability to find meaning and messages where the rest of us see only happenings, or yesterday's news. In this book, he and Patricia Ward Biederman make the past come alive again before our eyes, creating the "I wish I were there" feeling, but go on to draw lessons for life and work that apply to all of us, particularly to those who want to make anything of significance happen in their bit of the world.

The prose of these two authors is so seductive that you absorb their messages into your subconscious, learning without realizing. Too often in the past I have proudly produced what seemed to me to be a fresh nugget of good sense, only to realize later, shamefacedly, that I first read it in one of Warren's books. It will, I sense, be no different here. These stories of seven very varied but Great Groups are so vivid that the reader experiences a voyeur's intimacy with the individuals concerned. Yet with these authors' help the reader also learns, at one step removed, more from the experience than the participants probably ever did.

"Organizing genius" should be an oxymoron, a contradiction, desired but impractical, like herding cats. Bennis and Biederman, however, find fifteen clues to how to do it, nicely summarized in the final chapter, some of them surprising. The thrill of the game, not the money, is what matters it seems, making one wonder whether pouring ever more money over our managers is implicitly a confession that there is no thrill in their game. Talent, they also find, needs its own niche; roles in Great Groups are not interchangeable, so we may perhaps be ruling out the chance of greatness when we insist on interchangeability in our everyday work groups, in the name of efficiency.

Efficiency is, in fact, not a word much used by the groups in this book. Driven by a belief in their mission, unconcerned by working hours or working conditions, these groups aim to make a difference, not to make money. Could efficiency, productivity, and the desire for immediate pay-offs occasionally be road blocks on the way to greatness?

Those fascinating questions lurk behind Bennis and Biederman's stories of greatness. But the most disturbing questions they leave to last. Can the excitement of the task drown out any objectivity about its consequences—a question that particularly worried some members of the Los Alamos group that built the first atomic bomb, but only after their tasks were completed? In other words, do we too often let the means justify the ends?

Warren Bennis has been writing perceptively about leaders and organizations for decades. I first met him in a corridor at the Sloan School of Management at MIT thirty years ago, and he has been a formative influence in my life ever since, as he has been in the lives of many, many others. Courageously, unlike most professors, he has practiced what he preaches, as president of a great university. *Organizing Genius,* therefore, is a fine flowering of his own particular genius, a rich combination of his wide learning and his deep experience. Like all good books, it makes you think while you indulge.

Organizations are too often prisons for the human soul. This book offers a gleam of hope that parts of them, at least, could be springs of new life. I have relished *Organizing Genius;* others undoubtedly will.

Charles Handy

INTRODUCTION

This book was born forty years ago, in a conversation with Margaret Mead. Mead was already world renowned, as famous for her social activism as for her cultural anthropology. I was a newly minted assistant professor of economics at the Massachusetts Institute of Technology. One snowy night in Cambridge, I went to hear Mead lecture at Harvard. Afterward, I introduced myself, and we talked. I had become interested in extraordinary collaborations, the process whereby Great Groups are able to accomplish so much more than talented people working alone. I told Mead that I was interested in writing a book on how networks of gifted people have changed the world.

"That's a wonderful idea," Mead said, "especially since it's never been done before. You should call it *Sapiential Circles.*"

It would be decades before I completed that book on creative collaboration. During the intervening years, I became fascinated with leadership in its many forms and styles. I interviewed hundreds of leaders in dozens of disciplines, trying to pinpoint the attitudes and behaviors that allow some leaders to succeed while others fail. At the same time I continued to study how organizations cope with change, never more important than in the tumultuous present. The more I learned, the more I realized that the usual way of looking at groups and leadership, as separate phenomena, was no longer adequate. The most exciting groups—the ones, like those chronicled in this book, that shook the world—resulted from a mutually respectful marriage between an able leader and an assemblage of extraordinary people. Groups become great only when everyone in them, leaders and members alike, is free to do his or her absolute best. This book is about organizing gifted people in ways that allow them both to achieve great things and to experience the joy and personal transformation that such accomplishment brings. In today's Darwinian economy, only organizations that find ways to tap the creativity of their members are likely to survive.

The book itself became a collaboration with Pat Ward Biederman, a gifted writer who has been my friend and sometime coauthor for many years. As you can see, we chose a title other than the one suggested by Dr. Mead. *Organizing Genius: The Secrets of Creative Collaboration* is part history, part how-to manual, part meditation on why a few groups rise to greatness, while most flounder.

Warren Bennis
Santa Monica, California
November 1996

THE END OF THE
GREAT MAN

"None of us is as smart as all of us."

The myth of the triumphant individual is deeply ingrained in the American psyche. Whether it is midnight rider Paul Revere or basketball's Michael Jordan in the 1990s, we are a nation enamored of heroes—rugged self-starters who meet challenges and overcome adversity. Our contemporary views of leadership are entwined with our notions of heroism, so much so that the distinction between "leader" and "hero" (or "celebrity," for that matter) often becomes blurred. In our society leadership is too often seen as an inherently individual phenomenon.

And yet we all know that cooperation and collaboration grow more important every day. A shrinking world in which technological and political complexity increase at an accelerating rate offers fewer and fewer arenas in which individual action suffices. Recognizing this, we talk more and more about the need for teamwork, citing the Japanese approach to management, for example, as a call for a new model of effective action. Yet despite the rhetoric of collaboration, we continue to advocate it in a culture in which people strive to distinguish themselves as individuals. We continue to

1

live in a by-line culture where recognition and status are according to individuals, not groups.

But even as the lone hero continues to gallop through our imaginations, shattering obstacles with silver bullets, leaping tall buildings in a single bound, we know there is an alternate reality. Throughout history, groups of people, often without conscious design, have successfully blended individual and collective effort to create something new and wonderful. The Bauhaus school, the Manhattan Project, the Guaneri Quartet, the young filmmakers who coalesced around Francis Ford Coppola and George Lucas, the youthful scientists and hackers who invented a computer that was personal as well as powerful, the creators of the Internet—these are a few of the Great Groups that have reshaped the world in very different but enduring ways.

That should hardly surprise us. In a society as complex and technologically sophisticated as ours, the most urgent projects require the coordinated contributions of many talented people. Whether the task is building a global business or discovering the mysteries of the human brain, one person can't hope to accomplish it, however gifted or energetic he or she may be. There are simply too many problems to be identified and solved, too many connections to be made. And yet, even as we make the case for collaboration, we resist the idea of collective creativity. Our mythology refuses to catch up with our reality. We cling to the myth of the Lone Ranger, the romantic idea that great things are usually accomplished by a larger-than-life individual working alone. Despite the evidence to the contrary, we still tend to think of achievement in terms of the Great Man or Great Woman, instead of the Great Group.

But in a global society, in which timely information is the most important commodity, collaboration is not simply desirable, it is inevitable. In all but the rarest cases, one is too small a number to produce greatness. A recent study of senior executives of international firms published by Korn-Ferry, the world's largest executive search firm, and *The Economist* resoundingly confirms our thesis that tomorrow's organizations will be managed by teams of leaders. Asked who will have the most influence on their global organizations in the next ten years, 61 percent responded "teams of leaders"; 14 percent said "one leader." That does not mean, however, that we no longer need leaders. Instead, we have to recognize a new paradigm: not great leaders alone, but great leaders who exist in a fertile relationship with a Great Group. In these creative alliances, the leader and the team are able to achieve something together that neither could achieve alone. The leader finds greatness in the group. And he or she helps the members find it in themselves.

This book examines Great Groups systematically in the hope of finding out how their collective magic is made. We could have chosen any number of creative collaborations, from the artists who made up the Harlem Renaissance to the scientists of the Human Genome Project, but we decided to focus on seven that have had enduring impact. They are the Walt Disney studio, which invented the animated feature film in 1937 with *Snow White and the Seven Dwarfs;* the Great Groups at Xerox's Palo Alto Research Center (PARC) and Apple, which first made computers easy to use and accessible to nonexperts; the 1992 Clinton campaign, which put the first Democrat in the White House since

Jimmy Carter; the elite corps of aeronautical engineers and fabricators who built radically new planes at Lockheed's top-secret Skunk Works; the influential arts school and experimental community known as Black Mountain College; and, finally, what may be the paradigmatic Great Group, the Manhattan Project.

Why these seven? We chose to emphasize twentieth-century groups based in the United States because this has been a golden age of collaborative achievement in America. (As French observer Alexis de Tocqueville noted more than 150 years ago, Americans seem to have a genius for collective action.) And we decided to focus only on groups that have altered our shared reality in some significant way. The Manhattan Project, which ushered in the nuclear age with all its benefits and horrors, obviously fits this criterion. But so does, less obviously, Disney Feature Animation. Guided by an unlikely visionary named Walt, the artists at Disney did more than create an enduring new art form. The studio that Walt and brother Roy built continues to set the standard, both creatively and economically, for the entertainment and leisure industries worldwide.

All seven groups are great in several senses. Each was or is made up of greatly gifted people. Each achieved or produced something spectacularly new, and each was widely influential, often sparking creative collaboration elsewhere. To echo Steve Jobs, whose Great Group at Apple created the Macintosh, each of these groups "put a dent in the universe." It is worth noting that all but one—Black Mountain College—were engaged in creating something substantive and external to the group: a film, a computer, the first stealth plane. Groups seem to be most successful when undertaking tangible projects, as Black Mountain was when building its second campus. The project brings them together and brings out their collective best. When the thing is finished, the group often spins apart.

Given our continuing obsession with solitary genius, reflected in everything from the worship of film directors to our fascination with Bill Gates and other high-profile entrepreneurs, it is no surprise that we tend to underestimate just how much creative work is accomplished by groups. Today, an important scientific paper may represent the best thinking and patient lab work of hundreds of people. Collaboration continually takes place in the arts as well, despite our conviction, as the great French physiologist Claude Bernard observed, that "art is I; science is we." A classic example is Michelangelo's masterpiece the ceiling of the Sistine Chapel. In our mind's eye, we see Michelangelo, looking remarkably like Charlton Heston, laboring alone on the scaffolding high above the chapel floor. In fact, thirteen people helped Michelangelo paint the work. Michelangelo was not only an artist, he was, as biographer William E. Wallace points out, the head of a good-sized entrepreneurial enterprise that collaboratively made art that bore his name (an opinion piece by Wallace in the *New York Times* was aptly headlined "Michelangelo, CEO").

Other painters have worked collaboratively as well. In a landmark article titled "Artists' Circles and the Development of Artists," published in 1982, sociologist Michael P. Farrell describes the synergistic circle of French artists, including Monet, Manet, Degas, and Renoir, who pioneered Impressionism. Monet and Renoir often painted next to each other in the Barbizon woods. For a time, their work was so similar that

Monet had to look at the signature to tell whether a particular canvas for sale in a Parisian gallery was his or Renoir's. Braque and Picasso also had an intense creative collaboration, which gave birth to Cubism. For several years, they saw each other almost every day, talked constantly about their revolutionary new style, and painted as similarly as possible. They even dressed alike, in mechanics' clothes, and playfully compared themselves to the equally pioneering Wright brothers (Picasso called Braque, Wilbourg). Braque later described their creative interdependence as that of "two mountaineers roped together."

Creative collaboration occurs in other arts as well. Filmmaking is collaborative almost by definition. And Pilobolus, the marvelous dance troupe named after an unusually mobile fungus, began when a couple of Dartmouth jocks took a class from Alison Chase, a rare dance teacher who valued collective discovery over years of training. As one member of the pioneering group later recalled, most of them had zero dance technique to fall back on so they had to invent their own. "We definitely couldn't have done this alone," cofounder Jonathan Wolken told writer John Briggs. Writers, too, often reap the benefits of creative collaboration. The Bloomsbury Group is only one of dozens of such groups, albeit one whose antics have been chronicled at numbing length. Dorothy Parker and her vicious circle—the writers who exchanged barbs at Manhattan's Algonquin Hotel during the 1920s—is a home-grown example of a group whose whole seems to have been significantly greater than the sum of its acerbic parts.

Farrell's article on artists' circles begins with a quote from Henry James in praise of group creativity: "Every man works better when he has companions working in the same line, and yielding to the stimulus of suggestion, comparison, emulation. Great things have of course been done by solitary workers; but they have usually been done with double the pains they would have cost if they had been produced in more genial circumstances."

James's point is well taken. Gifted individuals working alone may waste years pursuing a sterile line of inquiry or become so enamored of the creative *process* that they produce little or nothing. A Great Group can be a goad, a check, a sounding board, and a source of inspiration, support, and even love. Songwriter Jules Styne said he had to have a collaborator: "In the theater you need someone to talk to. You can't sit by yourself in a room and write."

We chose our seven Great Groups to underscore the range of fields, including education, in which creative collaboration can take place. We also picked these seven because each makes a fascinating story. Vibrant with energy and ideas, full of colorful, talented people playing for high stakes and often racing against a deadline, Great Groups are organizations fully engaged in the thrilling process of discovery. It is our hope that everyone will be interested in some of these groups. (We have a nagging suspicion that we may have lost a few prospective readers by not chronicling a great sports team, such as the Boston Celtics of the 1980s, but we felt that was the one variety of Great Group that had been analyzed to death.) All such groups are engaged in creative problem solving, but the specific problems each of these seven faced and the solutions it found makes each distinctive. In the story of each Great Group, you will find the themes and ideas introduced in this chapter illustrated, illuminated, and expanded. But you will also find the brilliant answers to specific puzzles, such as how the Macintosh computer came to have icons that make us smile.

You might ask why we chose to focus exclusively on Great Groups when the majority of the institutions in which we work, teach, and otherwise participate are anything but. The reason is our conviction that excellence is a better teacher than is mediocrity. The lessons of the ordinary are everywhere. Truly profound and original insights are to be found only in studying the exemplary. We must turn to Great Groups if we hope to begin to understand how that rarest of precious resources—genius—can be successfully combined with great effort to achieve results that enhance all our lives.

The need to do so is urgent. The organizations of the future will increasingly depend on the creativity of their members to survive. And the leaders of those organizations will be those who find ways both to retain their talented and independent-minded staffs and to set them free to do their best, most imaginative work. Conventional wisdom about leadership and teams continues to glorify the leader at the expense of the group. Great Groups offer a new model in which the leader is an equal among Titans. In a truly creative collaboration, work is pleasure, and the only rules and procedures are those that advance the common cause.

Psychologically and socially, Great Groups are very different from mundane ones. Great Groups rarely have morale problems. Intrinsically motivated, for the most part, the people in them are buoyed by the joy of problem solving. Focused on a fascinating project, they are oblivious to the nettles of working together in ordinary circumstances.

Obviously, there are lessons here for transforming our classrooms, our offices, even our communities. Traditionally, collaboration in the classroom, for instance, has been taboo, condemned as a form of cheating. Yet what we discover in Great Groups is that collaboration can only make our classrooms happier and more productive. What lessons do Great Groups have for our workplaces, where so many people feel stifled, not stimulated? Look how hard people in Great Groups work, without anyone hovering over them. Look how morale soars when intelligent people are asked to do a demanding but worthy task and given the freedom and tools to do it. Imagine how much richer and happier our organizations would be if, like Great Groups, they were filled with people working as hard and as intelligently as they can, too caught up for pettiness, their sense of self grounded in the bedrock of talent and achievement.

Every Great Group is extraordinary in its own way. Yet all of them have much in common. Imagine that it is twenty-five years ago and you are a fly on the wall at Xerox PARC where the first user-friendly computer is being invented. The offices themselves are nondescript. But the atmosphere is charged, electric with the sense that great things are being accomplished here. Most of the members of the group are young—in their twenties or thirties—and each knows that having been recruited for this project is a badge of honor. Although Xerox is a corporate behemoth, there is no sense at PARC of being part of a major corporation. No "suits" from headquarters are in evidence. Instead, the atmosphere is much like that of a graduate department at a first-rate university.

People wear Birkenstocks and T-shirts. For the weekly meeting, everybody grabs a beanbag chair. Although the group is too busy working to philosophize much, any participant would tell you that he or she would rather be here than anywhere else. The money doesn't matter, career doesn't matter, the project is all. In some cases, personal relationships have been interrupted or deferred. It's hard to have a life when you're up half the night in the lab working on your part of a compelling problem, often with one of your equally obsessed colleagues at your side. This is not a job. This is a mission, carried out by people with fire in their eyes.

Great Groups have some odd things in common. For example, they tend to do their brilliant work in spartan, even shabby, surroundings. Someday someone will write a book explaining why so many pioneering enterprises, including the Walt Disney Company, Hewlett-Packard, and Apple, were born in garages. Disney's animators have often worked in cluttered temporary quarters. Black Mountain College managed with a leased campus during its exciting early years, despite the inconvenience of having to store all college property in the attic over the summer while the church organization that owned the buildings moved back in and conducted its programs. The Skunk Works did its clandestine work in a windowless building next to the airport in notoriously bland Burbank, California (the home of Disney Animation as well). According to late Skunk Works head Ben Rich, the place was "about as cheery as a bomb shelter."

We can speculate on why great things are often accomplished in dull or tacky surroundings. Perhaps a bland or unattractive environment spurs creativity, functioning as an aesthetic blank slate that frees the mind to dream about what might be. Maybe a great view and chic decor are distractions and thus counterproductive when important work is being done. But the truth is that most people in Great Groups spend very little time thinking about their surroundings. They have wonderful tunnel vision. The project, whether it's building the bomb before the Germans do or creating a computer easy enough for a child to use, is what's important. The right tools are essential, but fancy digs aren't. As a result, the offices of Great Groups often look, as Tracy Kidder writes of the Eagle computer offices in *The Soul of a New Machine,* "like something psychologists build for testing the fortitude of small animals."

All Great Groups have other commonalities. They all have extraordinary leaders, and, as a corollary, they tend to lose their way when they lose their leadership, just as Disney did after Walt's death in 1966. It's a paradox, really. Great Groups tend to be collegial and nonhierarchical, peopled by singularly competent individuals who often have an antiauthoritarian streak. Nonetheless, virtually every Great Group has a strong and visionary head. These leaders may be as patrician as J. Robert Oppenheimer of the Manhattan Project and the Kennedyesque Bob Taylor at PARC. They may be as seemingly simple, even cornball, as Walt Disney. They are sometimes outrageous in a juvenile kind of way, as Steve Jobs was at Apple and James Carville, the Ragin' Cajun, was during Clinton's 1992 campaign. But all these leaders share certain essential characteristics.

First, each has a keen eye for talent. Sometimes Great Groups just seem to grow. Some places and individuals become so identified with excellence and

11

excitement that they become magnets for the talented—think of the physics program at Göttingen that drew Oppenheimer and so many other great minds or the San Francisco scene that lured the writers of the Beat Generation. But Great Groups are made as well. Recruiting the right genius for the job is the first step in building many great collaborations. Great Groups are inevitably forged by people unafraid of hiring people better than themselves. Such recruiters look for two things: excellence and the ability to work with others. Computer pioneer Alan Kay recalls that Bob Taylor at PARC was a "connoisseur of talent" who recruited people both for their intellectual gifts and for their ability to work collaboratively. At Disney Feature Animation, head Peter Schneider also looks for both talent and the ability to work side by side, pursuing a common dream instead of a purely personal vision. Schneider doesn't want animators, however able, "who don't play well in the sandbox with others."

Being able to work with others does not necessarily mean fitting in in a conventional sense. Phil Jackson, coach of basketball's Chicago Bulls, treasures what Dennis Rodman brings to the championship team, despite—indeed, because of—his flamboyance. Says Jackson, who often uses Sioux and other Native American traditions to motivate the team, "Dennis has been a real blessing for us, because he's like a heyoka, the clown of the tribe. The heyoka was a cross-dresser, a unique person who walked backwards. He was respected because he brought a reality change when you saw him."

How do you find people who are capable of extraordinary work? Some leaders talk about looking for people "with fire in their eyes." Others rely on tests. Inventor

Thomas Alva Edison was both an intuitive recruiter and a systematic one. He liked to give job applicants timed tests containing 150 questions dealing with science, history, engineering, and other subjects. Believing that a good memory was the basis for good decision making, he asked everything from "How is leather tanned?" to "What is the price of twelve grains of gold?" J.C.R. Licklider, the psychologist who helped launch the Internet, trusted the Miller Analogies Test (the one that asks, "North is to South as blue is to . . . ?" The correct answer is gray.) Licklider believed that someone who did well on the test had a promising combination of broad general knowledge and the ability to see relationships. "I had a kind of rule," Licklider said. "Anybody who could do 85 or better on the Miller Analogies Test, hire him, because he's going to be very good at something."

The process of recruitment is often one of commitment building as well. At Data General, Tom West and his subordinates told prospective recruits to their secret computer project how good a person had to be to be chosen and how few were actually tapped. As a result, those who were brought on board saw themselves as an enviable elite, however overworked and underpaid. Kelly Johnson, the legendary founder of the Skunk Works, sought to recruit only the best person in each specialty the project required (Disney tried to do the same). As one of Johnson's lieutenants wrote to Tom Peters, "Each person was told why he had been chosen: He was the best one to be had. Whether it was absolutely true or not, each one believed it and did his darndest to live up to it."

Who becomes part of a Great Group? Participants are almost always young. In most of these groups, thirty-five was regarded as elderly. Historically, women have created some extraordinary groups. Consider the largely female coalition that mounted the New York City shirtwaist strikes of 1909–10. An alliance of woman labor organizers, teenage factory workers (most of them Italian and Jewish immigrants), college students, and a "mink brigade" of wealthy society women organized walkouts by nearly 30,000 workers from the sweat shops of the Lower East Side. Committed to collective action and social justice and dressed alike in white shirtwaists and long skirts, the women showed solidarity in the face of beatings, arrests, and, for some, economic ruin. Although their protest led to few long-term reforms and was overshadowed by the tragic fire in the Triangle Shirtwaist factory a year later, the action was a model of women working together to effect change. A number of participants were involved in other Great Groups. Strike leader Leonora O'Reilly, for example, was both a suffragist and a founding member of the NAACP.

Although women played roles in all seven of our groups, most of the participants were male, in large part, we can assume, because of lack of professional opportunities for women. Even when most members have been men, however, Great Groups are rarely stodgy Old Boys' Clubs. Typically, theirs is a playful, decidedly adolescent subculture.

We are deep in Peter Pan territory in many Great Groups, whether they include women or not (think of Black Mountain College under Charles Olson, who believed women made better mommies than poets, or the gifted but sophomoric engineers of the Skunk Works, who once had a contest to see who had the biggest rump). Although sexism surely kept women out of some Great Groups, there may be something in the group dynamic itself that has discouraged participation by women. (This is clearly an area for serious research, if only to find ways to tap the entire talent pool, not just the male portion.) Minorities have been under-represented as well, even at Black Mountain, the first non–African American college in the South to enroll black students and hire black faculty. Great Groups often tend to attract mavericks, such as Black Mountain founder John Andrew Rice, who was fired from Florida's Rollins College for bucking its president, and the irrepressible physicist, prankster, and future Nobel laureate, Richard Feynman, at Los Alamos. If not out-and-out rebels, participants may lack traditional credentials or exist on the margins of their professions.

Certainly youth can bring enormous energy to these enterprises, and not being a mainstream success can liberate an individual from too much respect for orthodoxy. But probably the most important thing that young members bring to a Great Group is their often delusional confidence. Kidder cites the recruiting strategy Tom West picked up from Seymour Cray, the legendary designer of high-speed computers. Cray liked to hire talented but newly minted engineers. He believed lack of experience was an asset, not a liability, because, as Kidder writes, these unseasoned recruits "do not usually know what's supposed to be impossible." The French composer Berlioz made a similar observation about fellow composer Saint-Saëns. "Saint-Saëns knows everything," Berlioz said. "All he lacks is inexperience."

Thus many Great Groups are fueled by an invigorating, completely unrealistic view of what they can accomplish. Not knowing what they can't do puts everything in the realm of the possible. In a radio interview, director John Frankenheimer, whose work includes the unforgettable film *The Manchurian Candidate,* said that the Golden Age of television resulted, at least in part, from his naïveté and that of his fellow video pioneers. "We didn't know we couldn't do it, so we did it," said Frankenheimer of making such classic dramas as "Marty" in a demanding new medium, live TV. Time teaches many things, including limitations. Time forces people, however brilliant, to taste their own mortality. In short, experience tends to make people more realistic, and that's not necessarily a good thing. As psychologist Martin Seligman has shown, realism is a risk factor for depression and its attendant ills, including an inability to act and the loss of self-trust. Great Groups often show evidence of collective denial. And "Denial ain't just a river in Egypt," as twelve-steppers like to say. Denial can obscure obstacles and stiffen resolve. It can liberate. Great Groups are not realistic places. They are exuberant, irrationally optimistic ones.

Many of the people in our Great Groups are tinkerers—the kind of people who, as children, took the family television apart and tried to put it together again. They are people willing to spend thousands of hours finding out how things work, including things that don't yet exist. There's a joke about engineers that captures the spirit of many participants in creative collaborations. An engineer meets a frog who offers the engineer anything he wants if he will kiss the frog. "No," says the engineer. "Come on," says the frog. "Kiss me, and I'll turn into a beautiful woman." "Nah," says the engineer. "I don't have time for a girlfriend . . . but a talking frog, that's really *neat.*" Members of

Great Groups don't fear technology, they embrace it. And they all think that creating the future is really neat.

Curiosity fuels every Great Group. The members don't simply solve problems. They are engaged in a process of discovery that is its own reward. Many of the individuals in these groups have dazzling individual skills—mathematical genius is often one. But they also have another quality that allows them both to identify significant problems and to find creative, boundary-busting solutions rather than simplistic ones. They have hungry, urgent minds. They want to get to the bottom of everything they see. Many have expansive interests and encyclopedic knowledge. Alan Kay, for instance, one of the wizards of PARC and now an Apple fellow, is a polymath accomplished in math, biology, music, developmental psychology, philosophy, and several other disciplines. During an interview with us, he talked insightfully about political discourse, economic theory, and the optimal size of a town before turning to his memories of PARC. Kay is the kind of person who says, with authority, "Computer science is a bit like a Gregorian chant—a one-line melody changing state within larger scale sections. Parallel programming is more like polyphony." Kay takes his insights wherever he finds them. What he knew about how children learn helped him imagine a computer that would teach them how to use it. A technique that Stewart Brand used in *The Whole Earth Catalog* to force readers to make a serendipitous journey through the book instead of a pre-planned one influenced Kay and his colleagues in designing PARC's revolutionary network browser. People like Kay are able to make connections that others don't see, in part because they have command of more data in the first place. It is one of the unique qualities of Great Groups that they are able to attract—people of Kay's stature, then provide an atmosphere in which both individual and collective achievements result from the interplay of distinguished minds.

The truism that people don't want to be managed, that they want to be led, is never more true than when orchestrating a group of Alan Kays. ("Knowledge workers" can't be managed, according to Peter Drucker, who coined the term. For that reason alone, Great Groups warrant close study by anyone interested in running an information-based enterprise.) The leaders who can do so must first of all command unusual respect. Such a leader has to be someone a greatly gifted person thinks is worth listening to, since genius almost always has other options. Such a leader must be someone who inspires trust, and deserves it. And though civility is not always the emblematic characteristic of Great Groups, it should be a trait of anyone who hopes to lead one. It was the quality that Maestro Carlo Maria Guilini thought most important in allowing the gifted individuals of the Los Angeles Philharmonic to achieve their collective goal of making truly beautiful music. "Even in delicate situations," he recalls, "I explained my views to the orchestra. I did not impose them. The right response, if forced, is not the same as the right response when it comes out of conviction." Those leaders of Great Groups who don't behave civilly (as Jobs sometimes failed to do, and Disney) put their very dreams at risk.

Members of Great Groups don't have to be told what to do, although they may need to be nudged back on task, as educators like to say. Indeed, they typically can't be told what to do: Being able to determine what needs to be done and how to do it is why they are in the group in the first place. In the collaborative meritocracy, people who are talented enough and committed enough are rightly seen as indispensable. The late Jerry Garcia, the great, gray presence of the Grateful Dead, once observed, "You do not merely want to be considered just the best of the best. You want to be considered the only ones who do what you do." Such people need to be freed to do what only they can do. Great Groups are coordinated teams of original thinkers. Kidder has a wonderful term to describe the structures that result in creative collaboration. They are, he writes, "webs of voluntary, mutual responsibility." Such groups are obsessionally focused on their goal. They could not care less about the organizational chart (which often becomes a dartboard in such a group), unless there is something on there that might get in the way of the project.

Our suspicion is that one of the reasons so many members of Great Groups are young is that, given a choice, more mature and confident talent opts for more autonomy, choosing to work collectively only when the project is irresistible. Disney Animation, for instance, is currently losing some of its best and most seasoned animators in part, Peter Schneider believes, because midlife priorities make creative collaboration less attractive.

Who succeeds in forming and leading a Great Group? He or she is almost always a pragmatic dreamer. They are people who get things done, but they are people with immortal longings. Often, they are scientifically minded people with poetry in their souls, people like Oppenheimer, who turned to the Bhagavad Gita to express his ambivalence about the atom and its uses. They are always people with an original vision. A dream is at the heart of every Great Group. It is always a dream of greatness, not simply an ambition to succeed. The dream is the engine that drives the group, the vision that inspires the team to work as if the fate of civilization rested on getting its revolutionary new computer out the door. The dream—a new kind of entertainment, a new political era, a radical new take on what learning is all about—is a kind of contract, a mutual understanding that the product, and even the process itself, will be worth the effort to create it. The dream is also a promise on the visionary's part that the goal is attainable. Each time Disney asked his artists to push the envelope of animation, he told them, "If you can dream it, you can do it." He believed that, and, as a result, they did too.

Truly great leaders such as Oppenheimer seem to incarnate the dream and become one with it. They do other crucial things as well. Psychologist Teresa M. Amabile and others have established that the way an environment is structured can have an enormous impact on creativity, for good or for ill. The atmosphere most conducive to creativity is one in which individuals have a sense of autonomy and yet are focused on the collective goal. Constraint (perceived as well as real) is a major killer of creativity, Amabile has found. Freedom or autonomy is its major enhancer.

Effective leaders are willing to make decisions, but they typically allow members of the group to work as they see fit. It was the director's skill at moving the project forward while letting each participant do his or her best work that art director Robert Boyle so valued in Alfred Hitchcock. Boyle recalls working with Hitchcock on *North by Northwest* (1959). From an art director's point of view, it was an especially challenging film because Boyle was forced to find ways around such obstacles as the Department of the Interior's refusal to allow Cary Grant and the other actors to be filmed in front of the presidential faces on the real Mount Rushmore. Having tough problems to solve was one of the pleasures of making the movie, Boyle recalls. (He was lowered down the face of the mountain and took photos of the sculptures that were then rear-projected when the climactic scene was shot back in the studio.) "Hitchcock was very demanding, but he was also the most collaborative of any director I ever worked with," Boyle said. "Since you were professional, he expected you to do your job. *He* made the unity possible."

Leaders also encourage creativity when they take the sting out of failure. In creative groups, failure is regarded as a learning experience, not a pretext for punishment. Creativity inevitably involves taking risks, and, in Great Groups, it is understood that the risk taker will sometimes stumble. CEO Michael Eisner says that Disney aspires to be a place "in which people feel safe to fail." An atmosphere in which people dread failure or fear that they will be ridiculed for offbeat ideas stifles creativity, Eisner believes. He often quotes hockey great Wayne Gretzky's observation that "You miss 100 percent of the shots you don't take." At Disney, Eisner says, adding an important caveat, "Failing is good, as long as it doesn't become a habit."

Although strong leadership is typical of Great Groups, its form may vary. The innovative and highly collaborative Orpheus Chamber Orchestra has no maestro as such. Instead it has different member-leaders for different concerts.

Many Great Groups have a dual administration. They have a visionary leader, and they have someone who protects them from the outside world, the "suits." Great Groups tend to be island societies. They are often physically isolated, as were the Manhattan Project in the New Mexico desert and Black Mountain College in the foothills of western North Carolina. While Oppenheimer was the creative head of Los Alamos, General Leslie R. Groves was its protector. Unloved by the scientists he served so well, Groves patrolled the border between the creative group and the exterior forces, notably the military bureaucracy that controlled the group's resources and could interfere at any time. Great Groups tend to be nonconformist. Their members sometimes dress haphazardly (Black Mountaineers dismayed the local townsfolk by wearing sandals or going barefoot). But whatever their appearance, they are always rule busters. People in Great Groups are never insiders or corporate types on the fast track: They are always on their *own* track.

As a result, they often need someone to deflect not just the criticism, but even the attention of the bureaucrats and conventional thinkers elsewhere in the organization. According to Kay, Bob Taylor did that superbly well at PARC. "Taylor put his body between Xerox and us," Kay recalled two decades later. The protectors typically lack the glamour of the visionary leaders, but they are no less essential, particularly in enterprises that require official sanction or that cannot realize their dream without institutional consent. This was the fate of the group at PARC. Taylor was able to protect his group from interference at Xerox, but he wasn't able to convince Xerox to actually put the revolutionary PARC computer into commercial production. In the Manhattan Project, Groves freed Oppenheimer to deal with the science and his independent-minded staff. Oppenheimer was able to get what he needed from the scientists, and Groves could get the scientists what they needed from the brass. Both men made the project a success.

The zeal with which people in Great Groups work is directly related to how effectively the leader articulates the vision that unites them. When heading up the team that made the Macintosh, Steve Jobs inspired his staff with the promise that they were creating something not just great, but "insanely great." He was able to urge them on not with a detailed plan for the Mac (which they were creating as they went along), but with slogans that reflected and reinforced the spirit of the project. "It's better to be a pirate than join the navy!" Jobs exhorted, and they raised a skull and crossbones over their offices. Leaders find ways to say or do whatever it takes to galvanize the group. When Frank Dale was managing editor of the now defunct *Herald-Examiner* in Los Angeles, he rallied his underdog journalists to struggle against the dominant *Los Angeles Times* by equipping his office chair with an airplane seatbelt. The message: The *Herald-Examiner* was taking off in its battle against the establishment paper.

Such leaders understand very basic truths about human beings. They know that we long for meaning. Without meaning, labor is time stolen from us. We become, like Milton's fallen Samson, "a slave at the wheel." Jobs and the others also understand that thought is play. Problem solving is the task we evolved for. It gives us as much pleasure as does sex. Leaders of Great Groups grasp this intuitively. They know that work done for its own sake becomes a wonderful game. No matter what our kindergarten teachers tell us, we are all Darwin's children. We love to compete. And so virtually every Great Group defines itself in terms of an enemy. Sometimes the enemy is real, as the Axis powers were for the Manhattan Project. But, more often, the chief function of the enemy is to solidify and define the group itself, showing it what it is by mocking what it is not. At Apple, IBM functioned as the Great Satan, IBM's best-selling computers as big, inelegant symbols of a reactionary corporate culture Apple despised. Jobs and his pirates took IBM on as single-mindedly and gleefully as a cell of teenage Resistance fighters going up against the Nazis. In Great Groups the engagement of the enemy is both dead serious and a lark. Thus in the landmark ad that announced the Mac during the 1984 Super Bowl, Apple tweaked IBM by suggesting that people who used its computers were Orwellian zombies, slaves to number-crunching conventionality. In a video reel shown to Apple shareholders the same day, a playful talking computer, obviously not an IBM behemoth, teased, "Never trust a computer you can't lift."

In the scramble to discover the structure of DNA, James Watson and Francis Crick cast scientific rival Linus Pauling as the villain. But nobody demonized the opposition to greater effect than did Clinton strategist James Carville during the 1992 presidential campaign. A master of memorable vilification, Carville heaped the kind of scorn on Bush and other Republicans usually reserved for people who do unnatural things to farm animals. Carville insists that every campaign needs an enemy in order to keep its energy high and focused. Leaders in other fields agree. In a dialogue with General Electric CEO Jack Welch published in *Fortune* magazine, Coca-Cola chairman Roberto Goizueta said that organizations that don't have an enemy need to create one. When asked why, he explained, "That's the only way you can have a war." In public, Coca-Cola may want to teach the world to sing, but in its corridors the motto is "Destroy Pepsi!" For the group, the bigger the enemy, the better. Great Groups always see themselves as winning underdogs, wily Davids toppling the bloated Goliaths of tradition and convention.

All leaders of Great Groups find ways to imbue the effort with meaning. Sometimes the goal is such a lofty one that the meaning is self-evident. Oppenheimer's group knew that its mission was the preservation of democracy. The scientists of PARC knew they were creating a radically new technology. But inspirational leaders can transform even mundane projects, turning them, too, into missions from God. It can be argued that the sale of Craftsman tools is not an intrinsically noble cause. But when Arthur Martinez took over Sears's retail unit in 1992, he recruited executives by promising them a challenge worthy of a Crusader. "I felt I had to be an evangelist," he told a reporter from *Fortune*. "I really was enrolling people in a mission." Turning Sears around, Martinez told prospective staffers, "would be one of the greatest adventures in business history. . . . There's no model for what we're gonna do. It's very risky. You have to be courageous, filled with self-confidence. If we do it, we'll be wealthier, yes. But more than that, we'll have incredible psychic gratification. How can you *not* do it?" Leaders are people who believe so passionately that they can seduce other people into sharing their dream.

People in Great Groups often seem to have struck a Faustian bargain, giving up their normal lives, if not their souls, in exchange for greatness. Because they are mission maniacs, obsessed with the project at hand, relationships outside the group often suffer. The wife of one of the engineers involved in Data General's Eagle project had no trouble believing her husband when he teasingly told her that the company offered alimony benefits as well as health-care ones. Inside the group, the intensity often has a sexual edge. Prosecutors Marcia Clark and Chris Darden had a romance, if not an affair, during the seemingly endless course of the first O. J. Simpson trial. As Darden subsequently explained, "We were working together fifteen or sixteen hours a day, watching each other's backs in court and commiserating over the media and other things no one else understood." At Black Mountain College, the passionate exchange of views sometimes became simple passion. Two of the school's three charismatic leaders, John Andrew Rice and Charles Olson, had affairs with students (Olson left his common-law wife and moved in with his lover, with whom he had a child). As Robert Cringely notes of Apple in its heyday, Great Groups are sexy places.

In almost all creative collaborations roles and relationships change according to the dictates of the project. In less distinguished groups, the leader would have a fair amount of managing to do. But Great Groups require a more flexible kind of leadership that has more to do with facilitating than with asserting control. Like cats, the talented can't be herded. The military model of leadership, with its emphasis on command and control, squelches creativity. Great Groups need leaders who encourage and enable. Jack Welch once said of his role at General Electric, "Look, I only have three things to do. I have to choose the right people, allocate the right number of dollars, and transmit ideas from one division to another with the speed of light." Those three tasks are familiar to almost everyone involved in creative collaboration. Many leaders of Great Groups spend a lot of time making sure that the right information gets to the right people—this was a primary purpose of the mandatory weekly meetings at PARC. Members of Great Groups may be so attuned to each other and to the nature of the task that they hardly have to speak at all, but they do have to have access to relevant data.

Leaders of Great Groups perform less obvious functions as well. Actor George Clooney, one of the stars of NBC's fast-paced medical drama, *ER,* says that one of the most important contributions its creator, Michael Crichton, makes to the show is his clout. As the author of one of the most lucrative entertainments of all time, *Jurassic Park,* Crichton is one of the entertainment industry's 800-pound gorillas. He gets whatever he wants. Clooney says he can name other projects that looked almost as promising and innovative as the highly acclaimed hospital show, but their creators had less juice than Crichton and their projects were eventually second-guessed and fatally compromised.

The best thing a leader can do for a Great Group is allow its members to discover their own greatness. But creative collaboration is a two-way street. Either because they lack the requisite skills or because the dream itself is so complex, leaders often find themselves driven by an aching powerlessness to realize their vision in any other way but collaboratively. Disney could dream it, but, in truth, he couldn't do it unless he got hundreds of other talented people to go along. The leader may be the person who needs the group the most. Luciano De Crescenzo's observation that "we are all angels with only one wing, we can only fly while embracing each other" is just as true for the leader as for any of the others.

Although Great Groups experience their moments of near despair, they are more often raucous with laughter. In the midst of the Clinton campaign, Carville took time out to crack eggs over the head of one of his colleagues, letting accumulated tensions drain away in an absurd but effective way. Epic company-wide water fights have become a fixture of life in Silicon Valley. Creative collaborators become members of their own tribe, with their own language, in-jokes, dress, and traditions. Apple became famous for its team T-shirts. Question: "How many Apple staffers does it take to screw in a lightbulb?" Answer: "Six. One to turn the lightbulb and five to design the T-shirt." Generations of Disney animators have seen how many pushpins they can throw at one time, the sort of mildly dangerous competitive play that the young have engaged in for millennia.

In a true creative collaboration, almost everyone emerges with a sense of ownership. In the early 1940s, students and faculty at Black Mountain built their main college building with their own hands (each student got to finish his or her room, with the predictable variations in workmanship). The Mac team expressed that sense of ownership by having all their signatures displayed inside each machine. It was a way of leaving their mark, of laying claim to a tiny piece of the new world they had created.

What keeps extraordinary groups from becoming cults? The fact that many are engaged in scientific enterprises may be one reason, since science, with its constant testing and habitual skepticism, is less likely than some other disciplines to breed fanaticism. Great Groups also tend to be places where dissent is encouraged, if only because it serves the spirit of discovery that is at the heart of these enterprises. These collaborations also tend to be collegial, with the leader perceived as one among equals, rather than as one in possession of unique skills or knowledge. Egos in Great Groups are often fully developed. Such individuals are unlikely to regard the person they report to as the Messiah.

Great Groups often fall apart when the project is finished. They are like animals that die soon after they breed. Why do these often short-lived associations burn so brightly in the memories of former members? Why does George Stephanopoulos look back on months of campaign drudgery and tell the president elect, "It was the best thing I ever did"? There are a host of reasons. Life in the group is often the most fun members ever have. They revel in the pleasure that comes from exercising all their wits in the company of people, as Kay said of his colleagues at PARC, "used to dealing lightning with both hands." Communities based on merit and passion are rare, and people who have been in them never forget them. And then there is the sheer exhilaration of performing greatly. Talent wants to exercise itself, *needs* to.

People pay a price for their membership in Great Groups. Postpartum depression is often fierce, and the intensity of collaboration is a potent drug that may make everything else, including everything after, seem drab and ordinary. But no one who has participated in one of these adventures in creativity and community seems to have any real regrets. How much better to be with other worthy people, doing worthy things, than to labor alone ("When I am alone," writer Carlos Fuentes says, "I am poverty-stricken."). In a Great Group you are liberated for a time from the prison of self. As part of the team, you are on leave from the mundane—no questions asked—with its meager rewards and sometimes onerous obligations. Nobody who was at PARC or involved in the making of *Snow White and the Seven Dwarfs* ever talks about the long days or who got credit for what. All they remember is the excitement of pushing back the boundaries, of doing something superbly well that no one had ever done before. Genius is rare, and the chance to exercise it in a dance with others is rarer still. Karl Wallenda, the legendary tightrope walker, once said, "Being on the tightrope is living; everything else is waiting." Most of us wait. In Great Groups, talent comes alive.

In writing this book, we depended heavily on existing histories and other secondary sources, augmented by interviews with participants in many Great Groups. This book could not exist without such superlative histories as Martin Duberman's *Black Mountain: An Exploration in Community;* Richard Rhodes's *The Making of the Atomic Bomb;* Douglas K. Smith and Robert C. Alexander's book on Xerox and the personal computer, *Fumbling the Future;* Steven Levy's story of the Macintosh, *Insanely Great;* Robert X. Cringely's Silicon Valley saga, *Accidental Empires;* Ben Rich and Leo Janos's *Skunk Works;* and the encyclopedic account of Clinton's first campaign, *Quest for the Presidency 1992,* written by a team from *Newsweek.* Tracy Kidder's classic study of a nearly Great Group, *The Soul of a New Machine,* was also invaluable.

TROUPE DISNEY

On July 24, 1985, Disney Animation hit bottom. That was the day *The Black Cauldron* opened to the worst reviews ever for a Disney animated film. The studio that had produced *Snow White and the Seven Dwarfs* (1937), *Fantasia* (1940), *Bambi* (1942), *Cinderella* (1950), and *101 Dalmatians* (1961) seemed to have lost the secret that it alone had possessed—how to make an audience care what happens to characters literally drawn into existence. It had been almost twenty years since the studio had produced the last animated Disney classic, *The Jungle Book* (1967). And with *The Black Cauldron*, an unhappy marriage of Tolkien and *Star Wars*, Disney had produced its first certifiable bomb.

"*The Black Cauldron* was the worst movie ever made," recalls Peter Schneider, now head of feature animation at Disney. Unlike the rest of the world, which has all but forgotten the adventures of Taran and his otherworldly pals, Schneider remembers the film vividly because it opened the day before he started at the studio. "The only grace I had was that I couldn't do worse than *The Black Cauldron*," he recalls with a laugh.

In the decade since then, Disney has soared to new heights. With its 1995 acquisition of Capital Cities/ ABC, it has become the most powerful entertainment company in the world. It has also created a new Golden Age of Animation. Since 1989's *The Little Mermaid*, Disney has released an unprecedented string of acclaimed pictures, including *Beauty and the Beast* (1991), *Aladdin* (1992), *The Lion King* (1994), and *Toy Story* (1995). Those films have added more than $5 billion to Disney's bottom line.

Once again, the studio that Walt built is making cinematic history. *Beauty and the Beast* was the first animated film ever nominated for a Best Picture Oscar. The wildly popular *Toy Story,* made for Disney by Steve Jobs's Pixar Animation Studios, was the first entirely computer-animated feature. Even less critically successful pictures, such as *Pocahontas* (1995) and *The Hunchback of Notre Dame* (1996), show evidence of the old Disney magic. Since 1989 Disney's feature animation department has again become what it was during its earlier glory years—a classic Great Group. By renewing its commitment to Walt Disney's vision, combined with a series of shrewd moves by the company's recent leadership, the unit has triumphantly reinvented itself, to the envy of the rest of Hollywood and indeed the global marketplace.

But in the mid-1980s the department was a mess. At that moment the entire company was in disarray. In 1984, Roy E. Disney, the son of company cofounder Roy O. Disney and the man Walt Disney sometimes cruelly dismissed as "the idiot nephew," had successfully ousted the administration led by Ron Miller, Walt's son-in-law, and prevented a hostile takeover by corporate raider Saul Steinberg. One of young Roy's first moves was to seek Michael D. Eisner, who had been the head of Paramount Pictures, as chairman of the board and CEO of Disney, with Frank Wells as president. As the duo began the drastic restructuring that would eventually transform the company, they took a long, hard look at the floundering animation department. One option was to shut it down. It stayed open only because Roy rallied both his persuasive powers and the clout of the Disney name to save it. Today, Roy has the best office in the company's whimsical animation building in Burbank, an office beneath the giant replica of the conical blue hat covered with stars that Mickey Mouse wore as the Sorcerer's Apprentice in *Fantasia*. It is the signature feature of the building, a symbol of the magic of Disney animation, and nobody deserves the office more.

It is only slight hyperbole to say that Roy Disney averted a cultural tragedy. Feature-length animation was Walt Disney's invention. Like the classic American entrepreneur that he was, Walt turned that invention into something that millions of people wanted and made it a continuing source of revenue for the company that survived his death on December 15, 1966. The animated feature remains a key factor in the prosperity of the international powerhouse that Disney has become, accounting for at least 40 percent of its revenues. As the father of Mickey Mouse, Disney knew that an animated character that captured the popular imagination was as close to a golden goose as a person could have. Mickey not only brought ticket buyers by the millions into movie theaters, but within a few years of the winning little mouse's creation in 1928, the character was moving millions of dollars of Mickey Mouse watches and other merchandise. As Disney biographer Leonard Mosley observes, Walt Disney exploited his cartoon character with the inspired efficiency of a farmer who uses every part of the pig but its squeal.

From a business point of view, one of the important functions of the Disney animated feature has been to produce a seemingly endless series of unforgettable characters, from Snow White and the Seven Dwarfs to Woody and Buzz, the digital buddies of *Toy Story*, and Victor, Hugo, and Laverne, the comic gargoyles of *Hunchback*. These characters cause millions of children around the world to lust in their hearts for Lion King lunch boxes and other paraphernalia, which adults eagerly buy for them to the ever expanding economic benefit of the Disney Company.

Disney stands virtually alone in its ability both to move its child-oriented merchandise and to involve adult consumers willingly in the lucrative process. What adult didn't know the Disney magic as a child? And so when *Pocahontas* comes along, you see grandmothers who were once proud owners of Cinderella watches buying Pocahontas backpacks for their children's children. With its theme parks (a Disney invention), its television network, its Broadway musicals and road shows, its retail stores, its publishing house, its interactive media division, and its ice hockey team (by no means an exhaustive list of Disney's many parts), the company has given new meaning to the term *synergy*, the process of orchestrating entertainment production, distribution, and marketing into a lucrative whole (a department of corporate synergy is officially responsible for that orchestration).

Perhaps what is most remarkable about this phenomenon is that the adults who do most of the buying do so not with a sense that they are being exploited, as they so often do when they purchase, say, a Mighty Morphin Power Ranger, but with contented smiles on their faces. The reason for this, of course, is that Walt Disney never created solely for children. When a man sitting alone at a recent screening of *101 Dalmatians* was asked if he had considered bringing a child with him to the movie, he answered, "I did bring a child—myself." The Disney of today woos this large and ever expanding adult market as never before. For every new animated film, Disney typically creates both a children's campaign, with a poster showing all the characters as if they were enjoying a party at summer camp, and an adult campaign. In contrast to the collective merriment of the juvenile campaign, the adult poster is moody and evocative—a good example is the John Arvin poster for *Beauty and the Beast,* which shows the Beast all alone in silhouette looking longingly at a single red rose.

Walt Disney believed in feature animation when most others doubted it was possible, and he went about conceiving and orchestrating the first and still, perhaps, the best animated features with obsessive genius. But from the start, feature animation was a collaborative effort. One of Walt Disney's self-serving idiosyncracies was to insist that he, like God, receive the glory for the studio's collaborative triumphs, while his cathedral builders remained anonymous. (As Neil Baldwin's biography shows, Thomas Alva Edison earned a reputation as a modern da Vinci by doing much the same thing, taking sole credit for inventions that were often the work of brilliant individuals and teams of individuals in his employ.) But even Mickey Mouse, with Disneyland the most purely Walt's of any of his creations, was a collaboration. It was Walt who decided in 1928 that his new cartoon character would be a mouse, and Walt originally provided the much parodied squeaky voice in which Mickey first speaks in the pioneering cartoon talkie "Steamboat Willie." But fellow cartoonist Ub Iwerks did virtually all the drawing, and even Walt's wife, Lillian, played a vital role when she advised him to name the charismatic rodent Mickey, instead of Mortimer.

As writer John Briggs observes, "Collaboration is one of the best kept secrets in creativity." Yet collaboration in the arts probably dates back to the first daubers of paint on the walls of caves. Even some of the artists that we most think of as lonely geniuses were actually the leaders of art teams. As historian William E. Wallace points out, thirteen people worked with Michelangelo on the Sistine Chapel and at least two hundred assisted, under the master's relentless scrutiny, on the Laurentian Library in Florence. Disney was working in a venerable, though rarely acknowledged, tradition when he created the Great Group that would produce the first animated feature, *Snow White and the Seven Dwarfs*.

For Disney, as for Michelangelo, the scale of the project made collaboration a necessity. Animation is one of the most labor-intensive art forms. Until the invention of xerography and computers that could be programmed to simulate realistic movement, an animated sequence that showed something as simple as a cow jumping over the moon required thousands of individual drawings. Even simple, eight-minute animated shorts were epic labors, and no single person could hope to produce a full-length animated film of any complexity. *Snow White and the Seven Dwarfs* would eventually run eighty-three minutes and require 250,000 finished drawings, not to mention the efforts of hundreds of nonanimators, from musicians to special-effects technicians.

The story of how Disney's *Snow White and the Seven Dwarfs* was made is a paradigm of a Great Group creating something wonderful and new. It starts, as such projects always do, with a vision. And originally that vision was Walt Disney's alone. As his many biographers tell us, Disney had taken a trip to Europe some time after he and brother Roy began producing popular animated shorts starring Mickey and his friends. There Walt learned that a Paris movie house was screening successful programs consisting of six or seven Mickey Mouse cartoons, shown one after another, without any feature film. But Walt wanted to do more than string short cartoons together. He wanted to make a full-length animated feature, and a great one, and he was sure film distributors would pay handsomely for it.

The fact that there was a compelling business reason for a feature-length cartoon does not begin to explain the achievement of *Snow White*. To get a sense of how far Disney advanced animation with that first animated feature, look at his own groundbreaking "Steamboat Willie." As delightful as it is, "Steamboat Willie" is a crudely drawn and jerkily animated little tale full of harsh sound effects and vaudeville gags. The movie that Disney began to make only six years later, in 1934, was not only longer, it was vastly deeper and richer. *Snow White and the Seven Dwarfs* would also be an unprecedented technical achievement.

Leaders of Great Groups often rally their troops with speeches in the mold of Henry V's before the battle of Agincourt. They promise their soldiers a terrible struggle against almost impossible odds. But the prize is worthy of each of them. It is nothing less than an opportunity to save—or change—the world. Individuals may fall in the battle, but their cause will prevail. Moreover, their shared struggle will transform them into a happy band of brothers (battlefields are always collegial, never hierarchical). Neither riches nor personal fame will be their reward. All the happy warriors can be sure of attaining for their sacrifice is the glory of the struggle and the knowledge that the world will long remember.

Walt Disney launched *Snow White* with just such a bond-building, going-into-battle speech. As his chief animators would recall years later, Walt warned them how difficult it would be to create, not just a long animated film, but a new form, full of drama and, above all, emotion. They would have to go where no animator had gone before. Walt told them, Mosley recounts, that "they would be called on to provide not just gags and comic tricks but the impression of fantasy combined with a real world full of real people doing believable things. Walt stressed that this would not be simply a cartoon film but drama, theater, with characters coming alive on the screen as never before in an animated film."

At first most observers, including his brother and partner, Roy, regarded the project as Walt's Folly. Among his detractors was rival studio head Louis B. Mayer, who thought the very idea was ludicrous. "Who'd pay to see a drawing of a fairy princess," Mayer asked, "when they can watch Joan Crawford's boobs for the same price at the box office?" But Walt was undaunted.

As psychologist Martin Seligman has shown, success is often rooted in optimism, optimism that may or may not be warranted by the facts. Great Groups are undeterred by obstacles and setbacks. Instead, they are buoyed by positive illusions that they can break new ground or succeed where others have failed. The leaders of such groups are purveyors of hopes, not necessarily voices of reason. The leader is often the one who believes most passionately. Walt Disney never doubted for a moment that he could make *Snow White*. His philosophy was both simple and inspirational: "If you can dream it, you can do it." His animators needed only to look into Walt's eyes to know that the project would succeed.

Often, the first and most critical step in creating a Great Group is recruiting. Disney wanted to fill his studio with artists capable of a more fluid, more realistic animation than had ever been attempted. To achieve that goal, he recruited 300 commercial artists, architects, and potential artists from across the country. The recruits were all male, since Disney believed that men made the best animators and that women had a special talent for the tedious, less well-paid jobs of inking and painting. (By 1942 Retta Scott, an animator on *Bambi*, had broken the gender barrier.)

Providing the training and other tools they needed to transform the world was the next step in forging Disney's Great Group. He began training both the new recruits and his existing staffers to be artists, not simply guys who drew glorified stick figures, however amusing. Walt began sending his staffers to night classes at the prestigious Chouinard Art Institute of Los Angeles, sometimes driving them back and forth in his own car. Later, he started an art school within the studio itself (the classes with nude models were wildly popular). He brought in guest lecturers, including Frank Lloyd

Wright, to share their wisdom about movement, the psychology of color, humor, and other subjects he saw as a fitting part of a Disney artist's education.

The ability to plan for what has not yet happened, for a future that has only been imagined, is one of the hallmarks of leadership of a Great Group, and Walt Disney did it as well as anyone. Of his educational program, Disney said, "It was costly, but I had to have the men ready for things we would eventually do." The program helped talented people develop the rarefied skills of a Disney animator, and it became a fixture of the studio. In 1961, Walt Disney gave $40 million to help found the new California Institute of the Arts in Valencia. Known as "the school that Disney built," CalArts has become the most important trainer of animators in the world. Its best students are regularly recruited into Disney and other studios before they graduate.

Like so many other Great Groups, Disney's was quick to embrace new technology and then to advance it. In 1928, "Steamboat Willie" had exploited the new technology for synchronizing sound with action on film. In 1932, Disney became the first studio to use the new three-color process from Technicolor. While the other studios took a wait-and-see attitude toward the new process (*Becky Sharp,* the first live-action feature in the three-color process, wasn't released until 1935), Disney immediately saw its aesthetic potential and began production of a color short in his popular Silly Symphony series. The resulting "Flowers and Trees" won the first animation Oscar, for best cartoon short of 1932.

Disney knew that color, with its ability to evoke emotion and enhance verisimilitude, would be a major asset in advancing his evolving art. In anticipation of *Snow White,* the studio made another major technological leap by inventing the multiplane camera. Hugely expensive at $70,000, the camera stood fourteen feet high. Like ordinary animation cameras, the new device shot down at a stack of artwork. But unlike other cameras, it allowed backgrounds, character drawings, and other individual elements to be placed at different levels, resulting in more realistic depth effects than had been achieved before.

It was the rule at Disney to act as if Walt and only Walt were the company. The people who made Disney's short cartoons received no individual credits on them until the studio-wrenching strike of 1941. In 1957, Walt offered an explanation of sorts to reporter and later official Walt Disney biographer Bob Thomas. "All these years," Walt said, "I've been taking the bows for the cartoons and the animated features. I did that for a purpose: to establish the Disney name as a guarantee to the public of good family entertainment."

If who deserves credit for what is often a question on a Disney picture, almost everyone agrees that *Snow White and the Seven Dwarfs* first existed, almost frame by frame, in the mind of Walt Disney. Nobody had to guess at Walt's vision of the film. One evening in 1934 he gathered his artists together in an empty soundstage and, under a naked lightbulb, he acted out the entire story. Sitting on folding chairs, the men saw and heard it all: Snow White's first encounter with the Seven Dwarfs, the individual foibles of the seven little men, the transformation of the beautiful but Wicked Queen into the cronelike Wicked Witch, the brandishing of the poison apple, even the final kiss that brings the comatose heroine back to life.

We are not talking here about a recitation. Walt apparently brought all the dramatic powers of an amateur Lon Chaney to the drama. The malevolent queen was the first of his many larger-than-life female villains, and Walt played her to the hilt. When he came to the part where the Wicked Witch offers the poisoned apple to Snow White, he pulled his coat jacket up over his head like the witch's hooded cloak and moved in on his innocent victim, the seductive offering almost palpable in his hand. When Walt, as Snow White, was awakened by the Prince's kiss, grown animators are said to have wept.

Walt's was no party stunt. The hours-long performance was the living script the animators turned to again and again as they struggled to complete the film. (It was not until the late 1980s that Disney animated features were actually scripted. Before then, they went right from storyboards into production.) Later, when Walt was trying to get $500,000 to complete the picture from Bank of America official Joseph Rosenberg, Disney repeated his one-man show during a screening of the half-finished film. Rosenberg made the loan, commenting, according to Mosley, "Pity we won't be seeing Walt up there on the screen. It's the best performance I've seen since Lillian Gish in *Way Down East*."

Americans don't like people claiming credit for other people's work. It violates their sense of fair play. And so Walt Disney was more or less forced to come up with a satisfactory explanation of exactly what he did at the company that bore his name. The Disney version of the truth, the one that the studio would turn to again and again, was the bee story. It appeared, for instance, in "The Magic Worlds of Walt Disney," an article on the Disney empire that ran in *National Geographic* in August 1963:

> You know, I was stumped one day when a little boy asked, "Do you draw Mickey Mouse?" I had to admit I do not draw any more. "Then you think up all the jokes and ideas?" "No," I said, "I don't do that." Finally, he looked at me and said, "Mr. Disney, just what do you do?"
>
> "Well," I said, "sometimes I think of myself as a little bee. I go from one area of the studio to another and gather pollen and sort of stimulate everybody." I guess that's the job I do. I certainly don't consider myself a businessman, and I never did believe I was worth anything as an artist.

Needless to say, when Walt received a special Academy Award for *Snow White and the Seven Dwarfs* in 1939, symbolized by one big Oscar and seven little ones, he didn't thank all 750 artists who worked on the picture.

But if live-action film is one of the most collaborative of arts, animated film is even more so. Most people cannot name a single person involved in *Snow White* except Walt Disney, but the movie required extraordinary work by hundreds of craftspeople. For example, the movie's most popular song, "Whistle While You Work," was composed by Frank Churchill, who also wrote "Who's Afraid of the Big Bad Wolf?" Snow White's youthful grace was based on demonstrations, live and on film, by a gifted eighteen-year-old dancer who would later gain fame as Marge Champion. (Disney continues to film live actors and dancers in appropriate costumes to inspire its animators.) People with dwarfism were hired to come to the studio to show Shamus Culhane and the other animators how Doc and his crew would carry their bodies on the march home after a long day in the diamond mine.

The group at Disney was able to generate and develop many more ideas than any individual could. One of Walt's most important jobs was to nix the bad ones and get the project back on track. One memorable example: Dopey—perhaps the real star of the finished film—was originally conceived as an old man, like the other dwarfs, complete with beard. But Walt decided that Dopey would have far greater appeal if he was young and puppyish. He was recast as a prepubescent boy and redrawn with the large eyes and flat, smooth features that psychologists now know elicit a sympathetic, protective response in adults of many animal species, including our own. He was also given baby-blue eyes (fifty years later the company would give the Beast eyes of "Paul Newman blue" to suggest with almost subliminal subtlety that something gorgeous existed inside the creature). In *Snow White* another significant correction was Walt's rejection of a series of truly awful names for the dwarfs. Imagine Snow White rollicking in the mittel-European cottage of Nifty, Thrifty, Shifty, Woeful, Baldy, Burpy—and Doc.

Like so many of the other projects described in this book, *Snow White* was a dream with a deadline. It required the coordinated efforts of hundreds of people working as well and as fast as they could. Principal animators, such as Art Babbitt, who headed the crew that worked on the bad but beautiful Queen, and Norm Ferguson, who headed the team animating the Witch, were able to do something that few artists in any medium can do. They were able to make drawings that stirred real emotions other than laughter. They grabbed the audience by the throat and scared its pants off (remember the way you felt as a small child, sitting in a dark theater, when you first saw the Queen go into her darkened chamber and begin her evil work). A vast collection of other artisans did their part as well, from the special-effects people, who invented new textured paints that made the Wicked Queen's robe seem velvety, to the sound men, who sang underwater to create the collective gurgle made by the Seven Dwarfs washing up for supper.

The decision to identify the work with Walt and Walt alone meant that everyone else remained in shadow, no one more so than Walt's brother, Roy. In the sometimes reverential studies of Walt Disney that have been published in recent years, Roy tends to appear as the man who tried to dissuade Walt from dreaming his visionary dreams, the pragmatist who tried to put the kibosh on everything from *Snow White* to Disneyland. In these accounts Roy's principal activity is saying no. But Roy was to Walt Disney what General Groves was to Oppenheimer during the Manhattan Project. Roy was the guardian, the protector who allowed genius to flourish. Roy played a crucial role in the organization from the beginning, not only freeing Walt to make creative decisions, but running the business side of Disney with great skill. Roy negotiated the studio's important distribution deals and allowed it to do business successfully in such new venues as television. Roy was also visionary in establishing links with department stores and other retailers to keep Disney merchandise in the public eye. For instance, Roy backed the establishment of Mickey Mouse Clubs throughout the United States during the 1930s. At their peak in 1932, more than one million children were enrolled in these clubs, which encouraged both theater going and buying Mickey Mouse merchandise. For better or for worse, a new Disney film has become as certain an occasion for child-oriented spending as birthdays and Christmas. And the credit or the blame for that lies as much with Roy as with Walt Disney.

Sometimes Roy did exactly what Walt's biographers say he did. He said no, or, at least, "enough." As other Great Groups, such as the Macintosh team, have found, at some point you have to deliver the goods. The process may be exhilarating, you may want it to last forever, but, eventually, you ship or you lose. One day, as the December release date for *Snow White* loomed, Walt discovered that the image of the Prince shimmied as he bent over Snow White's glass coffin. As Bob Thomas recounts in his *Disney's Art of Animation,* Walt told Roy he wanted to reshoot the sequence. But the cost of the film was fast approaching the then staggering sum of $1.5 million, and Roy would have none of it. "Let the Prince shimmy," he declared.

The still visible flaw didn't hurt the film's box office a whit. The movie premiered on December 21, 1937. It was the biggest film of 1938, bringing in $8 million—without benefit of Joan Crawford's cleavage. It held the box-office record until *Gone with the Wind* moved more tickets in 1939 and 1940. Moviegoers loved *Snow White,* and so did the critics. Westbrook Pegler declared it the greatest movie ever made.

A profile of Disney in his studio, which appeared in the *Atlantic Monthly* in December 1940, provides an instructive snapshot of Walt and his Great Group at their peak. The piece, called "Genius at Work: Walt Disney," is by Paul Hollister. While it stays focused mostly on Disney, almost to the point of fawning, it also gives a vivid picture of the collaborative process at the studio.

Hollister is masterful at describing the extraordinarily complex machine that makes a Disney film. The writer visited Disney's then-new Burbank studio while Troupe Disney, as he calls it, was making *Fantasia,* the most ambitious Disney movie of all.

Between 1935 and 1940 the studio had surged from 200 employees to 1,100 (roughly the number in feature animation today). The staff that Hollister found on the Disney lot was mostly male and mostly young—he put the median age at twenty-six or twenty-seven. They had been recruited from all over the world, with a single criterion in mind, one characteristic of Great Groups—that they were the best at what they did. "Disney goes after top men in their specialties," Hollister writes, "he'll be after Picasso, Grant Wood, and Ung [a Norwegian artist] any day now."

Hollister reported that Disney's staffers were a high-spirited lot, given to practical jokes. Although Hollister had the good taste not to make it public, much alcohol was drunk at the studio in its early glory days, and both football and croquet were frequently played in the corridors. On at least one now-notorious occasion, the high spirits got embarrassingly out of hand. To thank the staff for their heroic effort in finishing *Snow White* on time, Disney invited everyone to an all-expenses-paid weekend at a hotel near Palm Springs. The champagne flowed freely, someone jumped naked into the swimming pool, and soon the men who had drawn the Seven Dwarfs were cavorting with the nubile young women who had inked and painted them. Appalled, Mickey Mouse's puritanical creator grabbed Mrs. Disney and fled what came to be known as the Snow White Orgy in disgust. But blowing off steam, often in silly ways, is typical of Great Groups, a tradition that continues, with water fights and other merry pranks, in Silicon Valley today.

According to Hollister, all of Disney's 650 artists of the *Fantasia* period were specialists. Everyone was allowed to pursue his or her passion, and all Walt asked was that they perform supremely well. Hollister cites the example of Emil, a great animator who didn't do ducks. "The fact is," Hollister writes, "that this man can draw a magnificent duck. But Emil likes, he says, 'to futz around with big characters,' so it is Emil who created *Stromboli* and *The Giant;* it is Emil who created for *Fantasia* a devil who will scare the whey out of you. . . . There are Duck Men and Mouse Men. Top Duck Men or Mouse Men wouldn't 'feel' Emil's characters."

As Hollister rightly recognized, the ability to find a superb person and put him or her in the right niche was one of Disney's crucial leadership skills, perhaps the key skill of every steward of a Great Group. "To discover in each artist the caprice he best likes to draw, then to harness that specialty, is just one more example of Walt's determination to use the best available person for every task," Hollister writes. "One man likes pretty girls, reels them off by the mile, and gets miles of them to reel off; another thinks they're stupid. An artist espe-cially expert in facial contortions wails: 'They always give me the Inner Struggles to do.' "

Although everyone at Disney seemed to whistle while they worked, they worked like demons. Spouses and children were routinely neglected, including Dis-ney's own. As Hollister points out, perfectionism was the mark of the Disney staffer. The smallest things were done superbly. Hollister cites the forty-three separate sketches that were made of a baby rabbit, "a character of the utmost triviality," no more than an animated ex-tra in *Snow White*.

Whatever the job at Disney, it was approached with missionary zeal. Hollister describes the driven quality of the studio's sound-effects men and their sense of being part of a band of brothers, joined in the same single-minded quest: "You have a secret society of sound-effect men who can make a thunderstorm sound, not as a thunderstorm does on a microphone, but as a Thunder-storm With Personality *should* sound. They will work all afternoon for a proper recording of the word 'Hello.' They won't tell you or anyone else how they achieve their sound effects; they are jealous as panthers. They will spend several hundred dollars to construct a three-foot metal fan operated by electricity so that a singer may chirp a ballad into a glass lamp chimney and thence into the whirling fan, in order that his song may be re-corded with a certain querulous flutter."

We know how Disney chose to describe his role at the studio: Walt, the busy bee. In Hollister's view, there was perfect division of labor at Disney. The gifted staff-ers did their jobs well, and Walt wisely evaluated the results. Walt's musical director, for instance, "is a prodigy of musical expertness, and his ear goes to an error in recording as unerringly as a wet spaniel puppy goes to a light and costly Aubusson rug." Walt's job was curatorial, to recognize excellent work. As Hollister puts it, "Walt has no musical training and perfect musical appreciation." Disney evidenced a characteristic common among stewards of Great Groups. He didn't micromanage. He intervened after the experts on his staff had solved most of their own problems, not while they were struggling with them. The wisdom of this is palpable. It not only frees up the leader's time to do the things he or she can do best—inspire, communicate, and choose—it also gives staffers the sense of being autonomous that most gifted people require to flourish. Disney liked to tell his staffers, "Don't look to me for the answers. All I want you to use me for is approval."

Most of the people who were at Disney when the first great films were being made recall it as a singularly rewarding time. Walt himself said later, "Webster sums up the spirit of the *Snow White* enterprise in his definition of 'adventure': 'risk, jeopardy; encountering of hazardous enterprise; a daring feat; a bold undertaking in which the issue hangs on unforeseen events.' " As is so often true of Great Groups, Troupe Disney had the heady sense that it was inventing the future. The atmosphere in Burbank all but crackled.

Again and again, people who were there say Walt was the maestro who made the magic possible. "He had a talent to draw out of guys what they didn't have," animator Frank Thomas observes in Leonard Maltin's history of American animation, *Of Mice and Magic.* Jules Engel, now head of experimental animation at CalArts, worked on both *Fantasia* and *Bambi.* He remembers

Walt as a true artist who needed other people to express his concepts. But if Walt needed his staff the way other artists needed their paints or their marble, he never abdicated his role as creative director. Walt kept tight control over every stage in the artistic process. "Nothing moved," Engel recalls, "until he said, 'This is ready for the next step.'"

Walt had absolute faith in his instincts, according to Engel. "You could never sell an idea to Walt Disney. He came into a room, and he either liked what he saw or he didn't. And, if he didn't like what he saw, you started all over again." Walt had a gift for improving the work of his staff, studio veterans say. Even the most talented staffers usually accepted his suggestions, not just because he was the boss, but because, Engel says, "Every time he recommended something, he was always right."

An important aspect of Walt's leadership was to keep the staff's level of aspiration sky high. In Katherine and Richard Greene's brief Disney biography, *The Man behind the Magic,* a Disney animator recalls, "Disney had only one rule. Whatever we did had to be better than anybody else could do it." In Maltin's *Of Mice and Magic,* veteran animator Shamus Culhane recalls how wonderful it was to be at a place where "you could work all day, the whole eight hours, and at the end of the day look at what you did and put it in the wastepaper basket with no compunction. Nobody would ask you why you did it; they would ask if you *didn't.*" As to working conditions at the studio, Culhane makes an observation that applies to many Great Groups. "It was a very harsh place to work in," he says, "but harsh with every kind of advantage." The deadline pressure might be terrible, Walt might bark at you in front of your peers, but you had every piece of equipment, however pricey, you needed to do your job well. For example, every Disney animator had a Moviola for viewing and editing film.

Few animators left Disney, initially because of the paucity of jobs during the Depression and later because Disney was both prestigious and the only place to make feature-length animated films. But many also stayed because of their respect and admiration for Walt. In Mosley's biography, Nolie Walsh recalls how distressed she was when she realized that her talented husband, Bill Walsh, who produced *The Shaggy Dog* (1959) and other live-action films for Disney, was never going to strike out on his own. "Obviously, Walt had great power over him—as he did over all the vastly talented people in the studio's inner circle. The brilliant artist Peter Ellenshaw, a close friend of Bill, was in a similar situation. I'm sure that if someone had offered either of them six million dollars to leave Walt and go some place else, they wouldn't have done it. Walt had that charisma. He had very talented people who devoted their entire lives to him."

By the time of *The Black Cauldron* fiasco, Disney Feature Animation seemed to have lost its way. Walt had been dead for almost twenty years and had been preoccupied with Disneyland and other projects for almost a decade before his death. Most of the studio's most accomplished animators, the legendary Nine Old Men, were gone, and the studio's younger animators seemed to be looking to new, non-Disney sources, such as George Lucas's *Star Wars,* for inspiration. The studio had also been demoralized by the walkout in 1979 of rising star Don Bluth, who took a number of gifted colleagues with him and started his own studio. Another young animator, talented CalArts alumnus John Lasseter, joined Disney in 1979, but in 1983 went to the computer graphics department at Lucasfilm. Over the next decade Disney tried again and again to lure Lasseter back with the promise that he could direct, an offer few in the film industry can resist. Lasseter refused, because the Disney he left wasn't a Great Group; it wasn't changing the world. According to a colleague, Lasseter used to say, "I can go to Disney and be a director, or I can stay here and make history."

Once the new Eisner team decided to save the feature-animation department, the team made several critical restructuring decisions. It decided that the department would release a full-length feature every year, something Walt had dreamed of but had never been able to do. And, instead of having everyone working on the same feature, the group would break up into project teams and work on several films simultaneously. The latter decision was a particularly shrewd one. Disney has no competition, really, so how does it achieve that sense, so typical of Great Groups, of being a winning underdog? According to Peter Schneider, today's Disney staff competes against the giants of Disney's past, the people who made *Bambi* and the studio's other classics. But by dividing the department into teams, the studio created instant intramural competition as well.

To get animation back on track, the new leadership looked to the past and discovered that one of the company's greatest assets continues to be Walt Disney. Disney is a bit like the dead first wife in Daphne du Maurier's *Rebecca,* still a force to be reckoned with. The studio's eponymous leader is often invoked when the present leadership wants to rally its troops. Disney's name is clearly a kind of shorthand at the studio, a way to communicate a complex gestalt that includes everything from milestones in Disney history to the founder's insistence on excellence. It is almost as if Walt's successors have internalized him. Schneider, for instance, often tells new recruits what he sees as Disney's legacy: "Tell a great story, tell it with great characters, and always push the technological barriers."

The talented people who make up Great Groups are not easily led. Often, the leader's role is simply to keep them pointed in the right direction. At Disney today, Schneider says, management's role is to facilitate. Schneider sounds remarkably like Walt when he describes how he relates to the revitalized animation department. "At best I'm an editor," he says. "I'm an enabler, a sounding board." One of his most important jobs, Schneider says, is to tell people, "This doesn't work." And his biggest administrative challenge is "resource allocation," by which he means putting the right people in the right jobs. Like Walt before him, Schneider doesn't personally do the myriad tasks that must be done excellently to produce, say, *The Lion King.* Instead, he says, "I try to harness all these people into doing what they think is right."

The moviemaking machine that Walt Disney created sixty years ago is working better than ever today. And it is working in many crucial ways just as it did then. Of critical importance is that the studio continues to attract gifted animators. Disney created the feature animator, and now the studio can tap a talent pool that is often made up of people who have dreamed their whole lives of working for Disney.

That is certainly true of Andreas Deja, one of Disney's new master animators. Creator of the villainous Jafar in *Aladdin* and Scar in *The Lion King,* Deja also animated the hero of Disney's 1997 summer movie, *Hercules.* Deja remembers watching *The Wonderful World of Disney* as a child in West Germany, where he fled with his parents from his native Gdansk, Poland. "They would show clips of *Pinocchio* or *Bambi,*" he recalls in Bob Thomas's *Disney's Art of Animation,* "and there was this fascination, a pounding of the heart. Even when I was four or five years old."

Deja saw his first animated Disney feature, *The Jungle Book,* during the late 1960s. At ten he knew he had found his life's work. "For me it was just like a calling, like when a priest knows he's going to become a priest," he said in a recent *New York Times* profile. "You're hypnotized. You wonder, 'How is this possible, with these drawings? They think and they move.' I couldn't believe it."

To prepare for his vocation, Deja, aged twelve, wrote a letter to "Walt Disney Studios, America," asking how he could become a Disney animator (he had to look the words up in a German–English dictionary). He received a form letter advising him to work on developing his own skills at drawing animals and humans, not to copy Mickey Mouse and the other existing Disney characters.

Deja spent years grounding himself in the Disney style before he ever went to work there. If, as Peter Schneider says, resource allocation is one of his most important jobs, it is interesting to see how the studio first used Deja. As a new animator, but one who obviously had the potential to be a star (if Disney had stars), Deja was teamed with another young comer, Tim Burton, fresh out of CalArts. Burton and Deja were assigned to design and research characters for *The Black Cauldron.*

As Deja reminisces in the Thomas book: "Tim's designs were so outlandish and far-out, and mine were solid Disney drawing, so they thought, 'Hey, put these two together and something unique might come out of it.' It didn't quite work. You couldn't change Tim's drawings, really. They were great the way they were."

Burton went on to make two short films at the studio, "Frankenweenie" and "Vincent," before leaving Disney to pursue his successful career as director of such nonanimated hits as *Beetlejuice* and *Batman.* Meanwhile, Deja has become the consummate Disney animator, who regards work as play and who keeps the drawing board of mentor and legendary Disney animator Milton Kahl in his home studio. According to the *Times* profile, when Deja is having a problem with a character, he will sometimes leave a sketch on the master's drawing board overnight, "in case Kahl's spirit is tempted to solve it."

It may be a difference in temperament that explains why Burton struck out on his own and Deja, also formidably talented, chose to remain at a studio where the late founder will always be more famous than he. Awareness of such differences is critically important in creating Great Groups. Not every talented person can work collaboratively, and some can do so only when their contributions are properly acknowledged. And some talented people are simply disruptive. Schneider refers to those who unsettle the group as "people who don't play well in the sandbox with others."

Great groups exist when people of Deja's caliber can be brought together for a shared purpose. With a Deja or a Glen Keane, who created the Beast in *Beauty and the Beast,* there is no question that the assigned task will be performed superbly. As Schneider points out, "The artists don't give you something unless they passionately believe it's perfect." Nor does the fact that the Disney artist shares a collective vision mean that he or she (still usually he) does not shape his or her own work. Disney hires these people for their ability not just to draw, but also to infuse their characters with personality. Disney animators are, above all, actors. They know how to make the surface reflect emotional truths. Thus when Deja was animating Jafar, the wicked wazir of *Aladdin,* he found he could make the villain seem more menacing by making him move less. Originally conceived as a volatile Captain Hook type, who was always exploding with rage, Jafar was transformed into a still, remote, chilling presence. "All of the other characters in *Aladdin* are so bouncy, I decided if I just created this guy who watches everything from a distance, it created this dark cloud over all that bounciness," Deja said. He was also inspired by a former Disney executive. "There was something about the elegance of his lies, the smoothness, the oiliness, that I got into Jafar," Deja told the *Times.* "You've got to find a way to self-express. Otherwise you're just doing a mechanical job."

According to Schneider, the boss's key role at Disney Animation is choosing the best among the many exemplary ideas that are presented. Thus Walt nixed

Deanna Durbin as the voice of Snow White because he thought she sounded too polished and mature and opted instead for the sweet, thin voice of unknown Adriana Caselotti (he had the hundreds of auditions piped into his office so he would not be distracted by what the women looked like). The leader in such a group is able to say no or, "do this differently," because, Schneider says, "there's a collective consensus that this has to be right." Thus Katzenberg was able to bring about a crucial shift in the conception of Aladdin, according to John Culhane, who wrote the studio-authorized *Disney's Aladdin: The Making of an Animated Film*. Supervising animator Glen Keane had originally drawn Aladdin as a boyish Michael J. Fox type. Katzenberg didn't think a woman as beautiful and so-phisticated as Princess Jasmine would have any interest in such a boy and suggested that Keane revise Aladdin with Tom Cruise in mind. Keane drew an older, sexier Aladdin with Cruise's coltish charm and dark, eloquent eyebrows. (You can't help wondering if Culhane's 1992 account would have given quite so much credit to Katzenberg if the studio had known he would defect so disruptively in 1994.)

Although the spotlight continues to shine mostly on the people at the top at Disney, the new classics the studio has produced since *The Little Mermaid* are as col-laborative as ever. The jazzy Middle Eastern look of *Aladdin* was inspired simultaneously by the cartoons of Al Hirschfeld, Arabic calligraphy, Persian miniature painting of A.D. 1000 to 1500, Alexander Korda's 1940 film *The Thief of Baghdad,* and 1,800 photographs of Esfahān, Iran, taken by Rasoul Azadani, the film's lay-out supervisor, who grew up there. As in *The Little*

Mermaid and *Beauty and the Beast,* songs by Howard Ashman and Alan Menken greatly enhanced the film (Ashman died of AIDS before the movie was completed, and Tim Rice stepped in to write lyrics for several of Menken's tunes).

Another key member of the Great Group that made *Aladdin*—one who got no screen credit—was comic Robin Williams, who ad-libbed much of the hilariously manic dialogue of the metamorphosing Genie who advises Aladdin to "wake up and smell the hummus."

As it always has in Disney films, new technology helped make the magic. One of the most remarkable characters in *Aladdin* is the magic carpet, a Persian rug full of personality that was Disney's first fully computer-animated film presence. Before computers, the rug would have been far too expensive to animate conventionally, given the complexity of the pattern on its surface. The computer could make the carpet move, but the more basic problem of convincing us of "the plausible impossible" had to be done the old-fashioned way—by tapping the imagination and expertise of an animator. Randy Cartwright explains the problem in Culhane's book: "The carpet has no face, he has no voice, he has no body. It's sort of like acting by origami." Cartwright tapped into the studio's decades of accumulated wisdom on how color, movement, and other elements combine to suggest that inanimate things are alive and to make us care about them. Cartwright's salvation was the carpet's tassels, which sometimes hung at the carpet's sides like hands and feet and thus suggested where a head might be, a head that could be used to suggest an expression and emotion. The carpet was also brought to life through interaction with other characters, as when the rug responds with a friendly slap to the Genie's request, "Give me some tassel!"

Given Disney's penchant for new technology, the all-digital *Toy Story* might seem an inevitable development. In fact, it represents a real departure for the studio. Since a few ill-fated experiments with outside animators a decade ago, Disney has insisted on retaining absolute control of its animated features. But largely because of its faith in animator John Lasseter, Disney formed an alliance with Pixar, the Bay area studio that had evolved from Lucasfilm's animation unit. From reports in *Wired* magazine and elsewhere, it is clear that the Lasseter-headed team that made *Toy Story* had many of the classic characteristics of a Great Group. These include an atmosphere that *Wired* described as "raucously sub-teenoid." For instance, director Lasseter, who had left Disney for Pixar in 1983, had a wheelchair equipped with an oog-ah horn instead of a director's chair. (As Pixar's owner, Steve Jobs, former head of the Macintosh team, cut the groundbreaking deal with Disney. Jobs, who is *Toy Story*'s executive producer, became a billionaire briefly when Pixar went public and its stock soared a few days after *Toy Story* opened to raves.)

For years, Disney was notorious for paying its artists poorly. That, combined with anonymity no matter how great your genius, would seem like a formula for disaster. But Disney has traditionally been able to keep most of its top animators and other key personnel. Don Bluth, who set up shop in Ireland and produced such animated features as *An American Tail* (1986), was the rare exception.

Disney's past success at staff retention was obviously related to lack of alternatives. Until recently, there was no other game in town. Disney is, as Schneider points out, a monopoly (given the three-year lead time that animated features require, that is only now beginning to change). But the Disney hegemony was finally threatened by the creation of DreamWorks SKG, formed in 1994 by Steven Spielberg, David Geffen, and former Disney executive Katzenberg. There is now an animation renaissance under way, and several major studios are building feature-animation departments. Don Bluth, whose Dublin operation went under, now heads Fox's new animation studios in Phoenix, Arizona.

At Disney, animators' salaries doubled overnight in the wake of the first few defections to DreamWorks. But even before Katzenberg began gleefully luring top animators away, Disney was trying to find ways to retain key artists who were doing the kind of soul-searching typical of people at midlife, in or out of Great Groups. In Schneider's view, groups work best when organizational goals and personal ones intersect. Star animator Glen Keane, now in his forties, has long wanted to explore non-Disney projects. In a bid to keep Keane, the studio did the obvious and boosted his salary. But Disney made more subtle appeals as well, acknowledging Keane's unique contribution by featuring him at the annual shareholders' meeting and giving him a rare paid sabbatical.

In spite of front-page stories in the *Wall Street Journal* on the surge in feature animation, most of the people who make animated features still work at Disney and still do it anonymously. *The Lion King* was one of the most successful movies of all time. Can you name its directors? Do you know who animated Pocahontas? (See the bottom of this page for the answers.) Why do greatly talented people choose to remain part of a group that expects heroic achievement on their part, then works hard at keeping their names out of the paper? Not for the money, surely, even with bonuses and the promise of profit participation.

People work at Disney animation because they feel that they are part of something truly important, something insanely great. They work at Disney because, like the people who invented the personal computer and the people who got President Bill Clinton elected, they are on a mission from God. Hollister asked one of Disney's men in 1940 why he worked for the studio. "The thing here," the animator stammered, "is like that—you know, you can't help feeling that you're going to grab that goddam Holy Grail."

Answers: Roger Allers and Rob Minkoff directed *The Lion King.* The supervising animator of Pocahontas was Glen Keane.

A COMPUTER WITH
A REBEL HEART

Try to imagine the second half of the twentieth century without the personal computer. Less than twenty-five years after its development, it has transformed how we think, work, and communicate. Try to remember the original computers, so unlike the beige box and glowing monitor that now sit on the desks of 30 million people in the United States alone. The first computers were behemoths, so large they filled entire rooms, so expensive only institutions could own them, and so elitist they responded to commands only specialists had mastered. The punch cards that they consumed by the millions bore a message that summed up the clear and present danger of depersonalization they seemed to pose: Do not fold, spindle, or mutilate.

But by the mid-1980s the computer had changed utterly. It had evolved into a powerful but unintimidating small appliance for organizing and sharing information. It had become compact enough to sit on a desk or slip into a briefcase. It was benign, even playful. It was cheap, easy to use, even user-friendly. Today millions of us turn reflexively to our personal computers to balance our checkbooks, chat with people who share our oddest obsessions, write books, battle digital demons and supervillains, influence the direction of prime-time TV shows, research virtually anything, doodle, forge new careers, and send messages to our friends in the middle of the night. Not surprisingly, this remarkable tool—described by one of its inventors as "a product that has a rebel heart"—is the result of several Great Groups.

Its story begins, as developments that change the world so often do, with a personal vision. That vision belonged to Vannevar Bush, coordinator for United States–funded scientific research during World War II. In 1945, Bush published an article in the *Atlantic Monthly* titled "As We May Think." In it he proposed a new technology for managing information, which he called a memex. This new tool, he explained, "is a device in which an individual stores his books, records, and communications, and which is mechanized so that it may be consulted with exceeding speed and flexibility. It is an enlarged intimate supplement to his memory." The user of the memex could create personalized information "trails," using keyboards and screens to access and manipulate data stored in many forms. The user would sit at the desklike memex and travel through the world of information. Thus Bush wrote, as if he were able to look fifty years into the future, "The physician, puzzled by a patient's reactions, strikes the trail established in studying an earlier similar case, and runs rapidly through analogous case histories, with side references to the classics for the pertinent anatomy and histology."

Bush's visionary article was read by a naval radar technician named Douglas C. Engelbart, stationed in the Philippines. Inspired by the notion of interactivity at the heart of Bush's vision, Engelbart became one of the earliest champions of the computer as an interactive machine—not merely a superior cruncher of numbers, but a tool for enhancing the human mind. Encouraged by the introduction of computer timesharing, Engelbart established the Augmentation Research Center at Stanford Research Institute (SRI) and, with a 1964 grant from NASA, set out to make Bush's vision a reality. By 1968, Engelbart had already made two startlingly original breakthroughs in the embryonic art of personal computing—the mouse and windows.

Engelbart demonstrated his discoveries in the fall of 1968 at a national meeting of computer scientists. John Markoff described that landmark occasion in a *New York Times* article on the now highly evolved art of computer demos. Engelbart sat at a desklike workstation in front of several thousand of his peers and effectively ended the era of punch-card computing. "People were amazed," William English, an SRI colleague, recalled. "In one hour he defined the era of modern computing."

While Engelbart was able to dazzle his colleagues, he was not able to turn his pioneering insights and inventions into the first viable personal computer. Many reasons seem to account for Engelbart's limited success. SRI apparently regarded his work as peripheral; several gifted colleagues are said to have found him difficult and left his lab; and, worst of all, he eventually lost his federal funding. For whatever reasons, Engelbart's Augmentation Research Center did not become personal computing's first Great Group. That distinction goes to the Palo Alto Research Center, or PARC, a research and development adjunct of the Xerox Corporation.

Established in 1970, PARC would quickly develop the first user-friendly computer, called the Alto. As more and more of the country's best thinkers joined the staff, it became a place electric with ideas and the sense that the future was being forged there. Enlightened leadership at PARC enabled its resident geniuses to become a Great Group. But even its sophisticated leaders couldn't keep PARC from becoming a textbook example of how innovation can become detached from commercial exploitation. That story is ably told by Douglas K. Smith and Robert C. Alexander in *Fumbling the Future: How Xerox Invented, Then Ignored, the First Personal Computer* (1988).

But in 1970 nothing had yet been fumbled. Alan Kay was one of the first computer wizards asked to join PARC and, at thirty, among the oldest. At fourteen, Kay had encountered Bush's vision of the memex machine once removed, in a story by science fiction writer Robert Heinlein. The idea had fascinated Kay ever since, a thread that ran through his highly original exploration of biology, mathematics, music, and other disciplines.

In an interview in *Wired* magazine, Steve Jobs made a shrewd observation about creativity. "Creativity is just connecting things," he said. "When you ask creative people how they did something, they feel a little guilty because they didn't really *do* it, they just *saw* something. It seemed obvious to them after a while. That's because they were able to connect experiences they've had and synthesize new things. And the reason they were able to do that was that they've had more experiences or they have thought more about their experiences than other people." Exposed to art, music, and science from birth and a voracious and far-ranging reader, Kay had a vast number of experiential dots to connect.

In his doctoral dissertation at the University of Utah, Kay had described an interactive computer that would be easy to use and would "aid in the visualization and realization of provocative notions." FLEX— the name of both the machine and its language—was not technically feasible at the time. But it was a major step toward clarifying the mental picture of the personal computer that would eventually result in the Macintosh and in the millions of IBM clones that use Windows.

Kay attributes much of the success of PARC to Bob Taylor, who headed the most influential of its three component divisions, the Computer Science Laboratory. (Kay is now an Apple Fellow, based in Los Angeles, one of six or so individuals retained by Apple because they "have made extraordinary technical or leadership contributions to personal computing.") Taylor advanced the cause of interactivity during the late '60s as chief administrator for computer grants at the Defense Department's Advanced Research Projects Administration, or ARPA. (It was Taylor, when he was at NASA, who had funded Engelbart's work on the mouse.)

At PARC, Taylor's first and most important task was recruitment. He wanted to fill PARC with people with rare intelligence and creativity and to see how far they could push the boundaries of computer science. Often a Great Group begins with a great network. At ARPA, Taylor had come to know all the leading computer scientists in the country. Like Disney, Taylor didn't want people who were simply good. He sought to hire only the best. Kay says that Taylor believed, "You can't pile together enough good people to make a great one." According to Kay, Taylor was a "connoisseur of talent." He loved talent, and he believed he usually knew it when he saw it. "There were two or three kinds of sparkle in a person's eyes that he had come to trust," Kay says. Taylor's tendency to associate greatness with two or three personality types resulted in his missing some great hires, but not many, in Kay's view.

From the outset, Taylor maximized his chances of assembling a Great Group by looking for people who could work collaboratively. Taylor was willing to sacrifice the occasional disruptive genius for the good of a group who would enhance each other's work, not hinder it. He believed that collaborative skills were especially important in systems-oriented research such as PARC was undertaking.

At PARC, the selection process itself helped build the group. Candidates were not only interviewed; they also had to give a talk before the assembled staff and field probing, sometimes sharp questions and comments. It was a grueling experience, an ordeal, and thus a time-honored way of creating fraternity. Candidates who survived had built-in support from the others. "At PARC everybody had to want the next person to come in," Kay says. Existing members saw a successful candidate "as someone who was going to make it more fun for them." Acceptance was a high honor, affirmation that you were among the best and the brightest, and everyone was aware of it. "This is really a frightening group of people, by far the best I know of as far as talent and creativity," Kay said of the group in 1972. "The people here all have track records and are used to dealing lightning with both hands."

Recruitment was critical for several reasons. Taylor believed in the ARPA creed of choosing people over projects when funding research. Like George Pake, who headed both PARC as a whole and its science lab,

Taylor believed that good science was done from the bottom up. You hired great people and turned them loose on projects that reflected their unique talents and passions. They told you what they needed to do. The more easily the individuals interacted, the less distracted from their mission they would be. Collaboration was formally encouraged. "You could spend 40 percent of your time working as 'hands' on somebody else's project," Kay says.

The quality of mind at PARC was quite rare. Only the Manhattan Project among the groups in this book had a comparable concentration of genius. But any project that requires excellence creates a demand for meticulous recruiting. When Tom West was putting together his Eagle project at Data General, described by Tracy Kidder in *The Soul of a New Machine,* he did not have Taylor's luxury of assembling a creative dream team from a pool of talent with which he was long familiar. West and colleague Carl Alsing talked long and hard about whether they should recruit "kids," novice engineers, for the demanding project. They decided that it was crucial to hire people who knew more about the current state of computing than they did, even if it made West and Alsing feel superannuated. They had to be willing to hire people good enough to replace them, to be, in Kidder's term, "their own assassins." The confidence to seek out excellence is perhaps the first rule of recruiting and the one most frequently broken. Great Groups are always created by people willing, even eager, to recruit people more talented than they.

Because the talent pool at Data General was known only by its credentials, West and Alsing looked for direct evidence that candidates were suited for the project. Alsing thought one recruit would probably have a knack for writing computer code—a complex and creative task—because he had made a complicated metal sculpture. West and Alsing also sought candidates who were willing to "sign up," or commit themselves, by renouncing other involvements for the duration of the project.

At PARC, Taylor's strategy for letting creativity flourish was to "get really great people together and manage the social dynamic," Kay says. "Managing the environment was what he was good at." While at ARPA, Taylor had thought systematically about how best to manage research, finding take-home lessons in the behavior of project leaders he had observed in the course of handing out federal money. As Smith and Alexander write, the resulting model emphasized four things: recruitment, structure, communications, and tools.

Like Disney in its halcyon days, the Computer Science Lab had a flat, nonpyramidal structure, with all forty-plus scientists reporting directly to Taylor. This allowed Taylor to stay in touch with all the work going on in the lab, and it also freed the group from any distracting concerns about title or status. You were as good as what you were doing. The scientists could move from one project to another, which meant, member Chuck Thacker recalled, the best projects attracted the best people and "as a result, quality work flourished, less interesting work tended to wither." Taylor understood instinctively that he couldn't force the direction of such a high-powered group. He had to let his people do what only they could do, and then trust in natural selection to allow the very best ideas to emerge from the process.

Taylor offered his group a rare opportunity: the freedom to do basic research for a handsome corporate salary. But, for most, the money hardly mattered. Taylor had assembled a group of people who wanted nothing less than to reinvent computer science. A key element in Taylor's unusually capable and respectful leadership was communication. Sharing information is essential to a Great Group. The principal mechanism for doing so at PARC was the weekly meeting. These so-called Dealer meetings were modeled on the annual conferences that Taylor had started at ARPA, at which computer scientists with ARPA grants gathered to share their current research and submit it to the scrutiny of their peers. At these meetings a collective vision of the future of computing, including interactivity, began to emerge. (Kay recalls a metaphor from that era: "The ARPA dream was a magnetic field, and we were little iron filings lining up in that.")

Taylor knew better than to burden his gifted team with arbitrary rules. If some were arrogant, so be it. It was a small enough price to pay for talent (the attitude was pretty much "we don't care if they're prima donnas, as long as they can sing"). But the weekly meeting was mandatory. "There was only one rule not to be broken at PARC," Kay says. "There was one weekly meeting you had to go to, and you had to stay until the end."

Each week, participants grabbed a beanbag chair from the pile as they came into the meeting. At these often heated sessions, every member of the group was exposed to the ideas and fragmentary accomplishments of the others. Those "bits and pieces," as Taylor called them, were what everyone might have to build on in his

71

or her own research. Thus the weekly meeting served as a simple but remarkably efficient structure for exposing everyone to information that might prove key some- where down the line. The weekly meeting allowed information to be shared without resorting to time- consuming reports and memos. It also allowed tensions and disagreements to surface and be wrangled out on the spot. The meetings were a reflection of Taylor's un- derstanding of the dynamics of extraordinary groups. "No organization works beyond the size you can get all the principals together in a room and thrash out the is- sues before you go home," Kay says.

Taylor was also sensitive to the critical importance of his group's having the right tools. Most often, that meant tools they created themselves. In the ARPA community, everyone was both a hardware and a soft- ware person. "You had this group that was able to roll its own," Kay says. Being able to create their own tools allowed Kay and his colleagues to avoid the common frustration of having to work around the limits of inferior or inappropriate technology made by others. "Ninety percent of the code written today is getting around other people's mistakes," he says.

Cutting-edge technology is often a factor in the success of Great Groups, and PARC was no exception. Early on, the group faced a technology crisis, one that helped spark the group to greatness and also reflected just how far removed from the rest of the company PARC really was. Xerox had paid more than $900 mil- lion in its stock to acquire Scientific Data Systems shortly before PARC was created. It was Xerox's origi- nal intention to allow SDS to exploit any commercially viable discoveries in computing made at PARC. SDS had already produced a computer called the Sigma, and it was assumed by Xerox that PARC would use the advanced Sigma 7 in its research. But Taylor's people didn't want to use the Sigma. The SDS machine was inferior, the product of an outmoded paradigm, in the group's view. It was not interactive, nor was it compatible with ARPA software. The group argued that having to adapt the Sigma for its purposes would set its work back several years. Instead, the group wanted to buy Digital Equipment Corporation machines designed for use with ARPA software. SDS argued that such a move would undermine the reputation of Xerox's own product, the Sigma. It was an ugly battle that was finally resolved when George Pake threatened to quit unless the group was allowed to pursue a compromise and make its own computer. In eighteen months, PARC created a time-sharing machine with integrated-circuit memory. It was impishly dubbed the MAXC after SDS's Max Palevsky.

The willingness of PARC's leadership to battle the home office inspired enormous loyalty among members of the group. In putting himself on the line, Pake played the crucial role that General Groves had served in the Manhattan Project and that Kelly Johnson played at the Skunk Works. Most of the scientists at Los Alamos disliked Groves, who had a perverse knack for irritating them but who did a first-rate job of representing their interests with the governmental bodies they depended on. At Xerox, Pake, Taylor, and the other division heads were usually able to persuade the decision makers of the urgency of the PARC group's needs. This function is never more vital than when an elite group is doing something unprecedented and thus by its very nature is threatening to people who are more comfortable with what has been than with what might be. At PARC, Taylor, especially "put his body between Xerox and us," Kay says, still obviously impressed by Taylor's willingness to sacrifice his career "to protect his people." Taylor resigned from PARC in 1983 after being ordered to reorganize his lab along more conventional lines and to stop criticizing other parts of Xerox. He then set up a computer research operation in Palo Alto for Digital Equipment Corporation.

Taylor brought an almost religious zeal to his work of advancing the state of computing. Tirelessness, certainty of the importance of the task, unwavering focus—these were the qualities that Taylor brought to PARC and that he either recognized or inspired (probably some of both) in others. Born in Texas in 1932, the son of a Methodist minister, Taylor could talk about his work in religious terms. "Back then, people believed they were called to the ministry," Taylor said. "So I grew up assuming that whatever you did as a vocation had to have that kind of dedication under it."

Taylor had brought Kay into PARC to spark ideas throughout the organization. Kay had his own research unit in the third of the center's components, the Systems Science Laboratory. Here he was developing some of the ideas he had articulated earlier in describing the FLEX machine in his dissertation. The result was Smalltalk, a computer language that reflected his insight that computers were a medium, not simply a tool, and his belief that a computer should be simple enough for a child to use. (The computer that ran Smalltalk had a TV monitor for the display, a keyboard, and a mouse.) While many other computer pioneers had been preoccupied with the requisite mathematics, Kay was creating a whole new way of thinking about how machines and people might interact. His influences included the developmental and educational theories of Maria Montessori, Jean Piaget, and Jerome Bruner and the proponents of the Inner Game of Tennis and the Suzuki method of teaching violin. The computer that was evolving at PARC was a learning environment, not simply a mechanism for displaying and processing information. It would be easy to learn because most of the guesses you make on it turned out to be right. This notion of intuitive computing amounted to a revolution.

Kay's Smalltalk was the first object-oriented programming language. Another defining feature of computing today, object orientation allows the user to perform functions by sending messages to individual computational or software objects. The user need never be aware of the internal commands that are triggered by the messages. The defining metaphor for this innovation was the biological cell, which performs specific functions and communicates with other cells. However dramatic his successes at PARC, Kay says that his aspirations were greater than anything he actually achieved. Since seeing Seymour Papert's work with children and computers at MIT in 1968, Kay had wanted to develop an interactive laptop-type computer that even a child could use. It would be as portable as a book. (In conversation, Kay talks about the invention that helped democratize learning in the Western world. The ideal size had been determined by Aldus Manutius in the sixteenth century, when he scaled books down from the imposing size of most volumes then in libraries to something small enough to carry in a saddlebag.) Kay called his new kind of computer the Dynabook.

In 1977, Kay described the Dynabook, dubbed the most famous computer that was never made, this way: "Imagine having your own self-contained knowledge manipulator in a portable package the size and shape of an ordinary notebook. Suppose it had enough power to outrace your senses of sight and hearing, enough capacity to store for later retrieval thousands of page-equivalents of reference materials, poems, letters, recipes, records, drawings, animations, musical scores, waveforms, dynamic simulations, and anything else you would like to remember and change."

It would be fifteen years before the world actually had the powerful laptops that Kay imagined while at PARC.

When Xerox decided not to develop the Dynabook, the Computer Science Lab's Butler Lampson and Chuck Thacker began working on what would become the Alto, the first successful personal computer and the one that Apple, not Xerox, would ultimately develop commercially. The Alto had many of the features that are standard in the modern PC—bit mapping, which assigns a specific bit of memory to each pixel that appears on the monitor, a graphical user interface, and a mouse. The metaphor that controlled the design of the display was the desktop, Kay's inspiration in the direction of user-friendliness. Different tasks were represented on the screen at the same time, as if they were pieces of paper on a desk, in the form of overlapping windows. The Alto was revolutionary in another way, too. It was playful. The scientists chose Cookie Monster from *Sesame Street* to be the first image on their new machine. In addition to creating the Alto, the first-generation scientists of PARC developed the first easy-to-learn word-processing program, the first local computer network, and the first laser printer.

Although none of these would have existed without the coordinated efforts of thinkers of the stature of Kay, Lampson, and others, Bob Taylor was the maestro of PARC's success. "Without Taylor it would have been chaos," Robert X. Cringely writes in his popular history of Silicon Valley, *Accidental Empires.* "Bob Taylor's function was as a central switching station, monitoring the flow of ideas and work and keeping both going as smoothly as possible. And although he wasn't a computer scientist and couldn't actually do the work himself, Taylor's intermediary role made him so indispensable that it was always clear who worked for whom. Taylor was the boss. They called it 'Taylor's lab.' "

In Cringely's view, Taylor did nothing less than create "the ideal environment for basic computer research, a setting so near to perfect that it enabled four dozen people to invent much of the computer technology we have today." Taylor was the epitome of the leader as facilitator. He understood the wisdom of an observation that Xerox's chief scientist and PARC advocate Jack Goldman had clipped from a newspaper and hung in his office: "There are two ways of being creative. One can sing and dance. Or one can create an environment in which singers and dancers flourish."

The people who were at PARC remember it as the greatest time of their lives. "It was the only time I've ever been part of a critical mass for doing great things,"

Kay says. "It was the most fun I ever had." Chuck Thacker described PARC as "the largest continuous piece of creative output that I have seen anywhere. And it was like being right there at the Creation. A lot of people worked harder than I had ever seen, or have seen since, doing a thing that they all thought was worthwhile, and really thought would change the world."

In hindsight, it is hard to imagine why Xerox chose not to exploit the Alto commercially. Lack of vision at the very top of the corporation was one reason, but not the only one. The sense of being an elite team that flourished at PARC and energized its staff had a less attractive side as well. The PARC scientists were rude to, even disdainful of, Xerox officials whom they regarded as uninitiated in the mysteries of computing (the unanointed were sometimes called "toner heads," an allusion to the fluid required by the company's famous copiers). Bob Potter, who headed the computer-engineering facility that Xerox established in Dallas during the PARC era, was one corporate decision maker who felt the sting of PARC's collective scorn. "I went out there and I sat in their beanbags," he recalls in *Fumbling the Future.* "But I just couldn't get anything out of them. I even told them I was their savviest, best customer in the corporation. But they were only interested in their own thing. They thought they were four feet above everybody else. What the PARC people never understood was that they were supposed to help the less fortunate, less intelligent rest of the world."

What Xerox fumbled, Apple gleefully recovered.

The occasion was, as Steven Levy puts it in *Insanely Great,* a "daylight raid," conducted with Xerox's blessing. Xerox's money managers had agreed to allow Apple cofounder Steve Jobs and several of his staff to look at PARC's technology in exchange for a good price on a block of Apple stock. As a result, in December 1979—six years after the Great Group at PARC had conceived and built the first Alto—Steve Jobs and his coterie got a jump-start on the Macintosh. At a demonstration of the Alto at PARC headquarters, the Apple contingent saw the entire panoply of PARC breakthroughs, from pop-up menus to the mouse. Larry Tesler, who conducted the demonstration for PARC, was struck by the intelligence of the questions the Apple people asked.

Tesler, who later left PARC for Apple, told Levy, "It was almost like talking to someone in the Group. But better, because they wanted to get it out into the world."

Did they ever. Levy describes the scene. "Why aren't you doing anything with this?" Jobs wondered aloud. "This is the greatest thing! This is revolutionary!" On the short drive back to Apple headquarters in Cupertino, Jobs and the others talked about how they could use what they had seen to create a revolutionary computer of their own. As Levy writes, Apple now had the key component for building a new kind of computer: a paradigm. "By the time Xerox noticed they had the idea, it was already much too late. Apple had gone off to start the revolution without Xerox."

Although Jobs was cofounder of Apple, he had never been its technical leader—that had been Steve Wozniak's role. But it was Jobs who immediately understood that what PARC had developed was the future of computing. As he told *Wired* magazine in 1996, "When I went to Xerox PARC in 1979, I saw a very rudimentary graphical user interface. It wasn't complete. It wasn't quite right. But within 10 minutes, it was obvious that every computer in the world would work this way someday."

Jobs's genius had always been for marketing the products made by Wozniak and the others. Now he had a vision of his own—granted, not an original vision, but one that he could take ownership of. All he needed to do was to build the machine, market it in his own inimitable fashion, and get it shipped. The story of the Macintosh is now a Silicon Valley legend: how Jobs forced Jef Raskin out of the existing Macintosh project and put his own brilliant and adolescent stamp on it; how he gathered a small group of talented programmers, designers, and marketers and alternately inspired them and bullied them into making something "insanely great"; how he instilled in his Great Group the sense that they were a supremely gifted band of rebels, taking on other project teams within Apple as well as the rest of the digital world.

Apple, which started in the mid-1970s in a garage, was famous for its freewheeling atmosphere, even as the company grew and became more corporate. As the head of the Macintosh team, Jobs succeeded in imbuing his group with some of the original Apple spirit. They moved into their own building, Bandley 3, and began working 100-hour weeks. Jobs promised them they were going to build a machine that would "put a dent in the universe." They were not engineers or marketers, they were buccaneers, cunning underdogs, going up against the Establishment in the name of excellence and innovation. "It's better to be a pirate than join the navy!" Jobs urged in one of his trademark epigrams, and they raised a skull and crossbones over Bandley.

Jobs had a genius for building group identity. He handed out distinctive T-shirts and offered such childish but effective incentives as buying pineapple pizza for everyone if they completed a particularly difficult task by a certain time. He shrouded their work in mystery, insisting that no outsider be told what they were up to. The Macintosh was their Manhattan Project, their Skunk Works—a secret project of life-changing importance. Secrecy has long been a passion of Great Groups. Whether national security requires it or not, secrecy serves to distinguish those who know from those who don't, binding the insiders that much closer together.

It is instructive to compare Jobs's leadership at Apple with Taylor's at PARC. Taylor was no saint. He tended to have a binary view of people. As one of the men who worked under him said, "Taylor only had two modes: either you were the greatest thing that ever walked the earth or you were scum." But Taylor never abused the members of his group, as Jobs did at Apple. Jobs was notorious for what the people who suffered it called Management by Walking Around. He would suddenly appear in Bandley, looking at people's work and making scathing comments, even when he had no relevant expertise. "This sucks!" was a favorite Jobsian critique.

Jobs was only twenty-four when he found the paradigm of a lifetime at PARC. His youth and that of other Apple staff prompted the joke, "What's the difference between Apple and the Boy Scouts?" Answer: "The Boy Scouts have adult supervision." Perhaps Jobs should simply be forgiven for what can most kindly be described as an immature leadership style. But his behavior clearly undermined his authority. According to Levy, Jobs's team routinely joked about the Reality Distortion Field he carried around with him. Behind his back, they often did whatever they thought best, as when they added the capacity for additional memory to the woefully underequipped Mac. What was the real cost of Jobs's uncivil behavior? How much did he slow down the Mac effort, instead of advancing it, by ratcheting up the stress level? How much time and emotional energy did team members lose to bracing for surprise attacks from their leader? Decency in the workplace, especially one that depends for its success on the talent and devotion of its employees, isn't just the right thing to do. It's the *smart* thing to do. The talent is your treasure. You don't chew it up.

Among the major talents on the Mac team was Susan Kare. A defining feature of the Macintosh is that it has a personality, and much of the credit for that goes to Kare, who designed its famous garbage can and other icons. Kare's expertise was very different from the programming and engineering skills of most of her colleagues. Brought into the project by Andy Hertzfeld, whom she knew from high school, Kare had a doctorate in fine arts. She also has a gift for an art form that she all but invented—designing the pinky-sized images of typewriters and other objects that users of computers with graphical interfaces point to and click on. Kare, who now has her own studio in San Francisco, designed the Mac's typefaces as well as its icons. After leaving Apple, she created a series of whimsical icons for rival Microsoft's Windows 3.0.

Jobs made critical contributions to the development of the Mac, including insisting on its elegant design. Bill Gates has said that the Mac would never have existed without Jobs, and Kay paid him the compliment of saying that his personal computer was the "first worth criticizing" (which Kay, already an Apple Fellow, did in a 1984 memo titled "Would You Buy a Honda with a One-Gallon Gas Tank?").

Much has been made of the fact that people on the Mac team worked with fire in their eyes. How much of that was attributable to Jobs, and how much of it was the intrinsic pleasure associated with doing something challenging and important probably doesn't matter. "Everyone who worked there identified totally with their work—we all believed we were on a mission from God," Randy Wigginton said afterwards. Everyone on the team had invested a part of himself or herself in this first lovable computer. In an act that symbolized their creative collaboration, the Mac group wrote their signatures for a little plate to be installed inside each machine. They would know it was there even if no one else ever saw it.

The first Macintoshes shipped in 1984, years later than anyone who had been with Jobs at the Alto demonstration in 1979 would have predicted. Nor was the Macintosh a great commercial success initially. But the people who made the Mac were as proud of their involvement in the project as the people who made *Bambi* were of theirs. Steve Capps said the Mac experience was "the best thing I ever did in my life." Andy Hertzfeld told Levy: "We never doubted that the way we did things would catch on. The key thing is that we kept the Apple II spirit, the crazy irreverence, the anti-authority flavor. Macintosh tells people as they use it, 'You don't have to take things too seriously.' It was great to make a product that has a rebel heart."

Steve Jobs once wrote on an easel during one of his pep talks, "The journey is the reward." Lofty goals, great ambition, a sense of being the best and having the potential to change the world often transmogrifies a Great Group's relentless labor into something remembered as golden, even when conditions are harsh. Commercial success doesn't have to be part of the equation. Most members of the Great Group at PARC do not seem unduly distressed that their work led only to the Macs and Windows-driven PCs that are everywhere today. In part, that reflects the fact that the members of the PARC group saw themselves primarily as scientists. And as Alan Kay says, "The main difference between scientists and engineers is that engineers want to make things and scientists want to understand them." The PARC people wanted to understand how information could be stored and transferred and manipulated as never before, and, to a remarkable degree, they succeeded. The Mac people wanted to make—and ship—an insanely great machine. They succeeded as well.

But at Apple the price was high. Marriages and other relationships floundered under the pressure. The Mac team was exhausted by the time they got their machine out the door. They simply didn't have the energy to make the fixes the computer needed or to start other projects. Some left the company. The relentless fervor that Jobs brought to creating and promoting the Mac seems to have been most effective—and least destructive—when exercised at a distance. If you actually worked for Jobs, he took time out from preaching the Mac gospel to meddle in your life. For example, he started the practice of having Apple employees share rooms when they were at conventions and other professional meetings. The reason, according to Cringely, was "to limit bed hopping, not to save money. Apple is a very sexy company, and Jobs wanted his people to lavish that libido on the products rather than on each other."

A wiser, less self-centered leader would have known that the Mac team was headed for a postpartum depression of epic proportions and would have tried to ease the pain, as West did at Data General. Indifferent or oblivious, Jobs busied himself presenting Macs to Andy Warhol, Mick Jagger, and other celebrities.

In his forties, Jobs seems to have mellowed, as a leader if not as a crusader for Mac-style computing. As head of NeXT Software and of Pixar, the computer-animation firm that scored big with *Toy Story,* Jobs is still a visionary, but he seems to have learned how to lead without bullying. Jobs gives the lie to F. Scott Fitzgerald's observation that there are no second acts in American life. Since leaving Apple, Jobs has found another niche and even remade the fortune, thanks to Pixar stock, that he lost when he angrily unloaded his depressed Apple shares a decade ago. As a corporate leader, Jobs no longer seems bent on turning the workplace into a dysfunctional family with an abusive head. And Jobs's message is still resonant. Today the Macintosh is both a computer and a secular religion. In a poignant piece in the *New York Times,* Mac user Lloyd Krieger described his life with the machine and expressed the hope that he would never have to give up this symbol of his youthful, rebellious creativity for a clunky old PC, even if it is cheaper and comes with more software. Why would anybody switch to Windows 95 when he or she could have a real Mac? Krieger wondered. "Why listen to Harry Connick Jr. when you can listen to Frank Sinatra?"

Although Jobs was ousted from Apple in 1985, his vision of the Macintosh as a cause and not simply a product may save the troubled company yet. Apple has hired back Guy Kawasaki, who was one of Jobs's original "evangelists" (that was the title on their business cards), as one of its half-dozen Apple Fellows. Kawasaki's mission, which he has accepted, is to keep the Apple cult alive. Kawasaki spreads Good News about the Mac in such forums as an Internet newsletter, where the standard Apple response to Windows 95 is "Been there. . . done that." "My goal," Kawasaki says, "is to carry the Macintosh torch and save computer users from the gates of hell." Jobs couldn't have said it better himself.

What PARC dreamed of and developed on a limited scale, Apple sent out into the world, thanks to Steve Jobs. In one of the great ironies of computer history, Jobs once charged Bill Gates, whose Windows software makes every computer a watered-down Mac, with lifting Apple's ideas. "No, Steve," Gates countered, "I think it's more like we both have this rich neighbor named Xerox, and you broke in to steal the TV set, found I'd been there first, and said, 'No fair, I wanted to steal the TV set!' "

SELLING A PLACE
CALLED HOPE

No process is more collaborative than the one that puts a person in the White House. For more than a year, hundreds of people worked to bring about Bill Clinton's remarkable victory in 1992. From the charismatic candidate himself to Democratic Party chief Ron Brown, this Great Group included Clinton's able and committed wife, Hillary Rodham Clinton; political strategists; fund-raisers; pollsters; and, in Paul Begala, a gifted and nimble speechwriter who wrote moving, even soaring, lines for Clinton in a campaign that was marked by more rancor and mudslinging than any other in recent times. Clinton's very decision to run was collaborative, the result of an over-the-pillow conversation with his wife in the summer of 1991.

Bill Clinton is a man of unusual intelligence, a former Rhodes scholar who still remembers the phone numbers of his college friends. He is a large, handsome man, who seems to supercharge any room he enters. But he was far from a shoo-in for president. The Republicans had dominated presidential politics for almost twenty-five years when Clinton began his bid for the White House. Clinton was young, only forty-five when the race began, and known, if he was known at all, as the governor of the relatively poor, relatively obscure state of Arkansas. The race was an especially tough one. He first had to win his party's nomination in a crowded field of six. He then faced an incumbent president, George Bush, who, in the aftermath of the Persian Gulf War, was viewed favorably by a staggering 91 percent of the populace. Ross Perot, the third-party candidate with big ears, a big ego, and a big budget, presented an additional complication. Perot would spend $60 million on advertising—much of it his own money—in the course of his seriocomic run for the highest office in the land.

Some observers say Bill Clinton had been preparing for the presidency his entire life. They point to such formative experiences as his meeting, as a sixteen-year-old student politician, with his hero, President John F. Kennedy, on the White House lawn. But Clinton's run for the presidency really began to take shape in the mid-1980s, when he helped found the Democratic Leadership Council. Made up of many of the party's best and brightest, the council was seeking a way to break the Republican lock on the White House. And the council was also redefining what it meant to be a Democrat, a member of a party that had once embodied the belief that government could be a force for good in people's lives but that seemed to have lost its way since the glory days of FDR and the thousand days of Kennedy's Camelot.

A new centrism was the defining characteristic of the party reinvented by the Democratic Leadership Council. In May of 1991, Clinton, a former chair of the group, created a buzz at its annual convention in Cleveland with an address that seemed to sum up the new hopefulness of this activist wing of the party. "His text amounted to a manifesto for a postmodern Democratic politics, beyond the stale old contention between liberal and conservative," write the authors of *Quest for the Presidency 1992*. "The choice that counted was between yesterday and tomorrow, he argued, and the party's future lay in getting on the right side of the equation."

In many ways, Clinton is a child of his times. He loves rock 'n' roll (his staff called him by the code name Elvis during the campaign). He also shares many of the other values of his post–World War II baby-boom generation. One of these is respect for collective action, gained in the late '60s and early '70s, when indignant students, working together, closed down their campuses to protest what they regarded as an immoral war. In a very real sense, Clinton is the first "Big Chill" president, the first to have seriously considered communal living, the first to have been steeped in the post-1960s process of learning and making decisions in groups. As his commitment to an annual group think-fest, the Renaissance Weekend, suggests, Clinton is highly collaborative. By temperament and training, he was prepared to put together a Great Group to help him win the presidency. An inveterate networker, Clinton has religiously cultivated his Rolodex since his student days at Georgetown University, Yale, and Oxford. He knew he would need first-rate professionals if he wanted to win this election, and he knew where to find them.

There is a certain kind of leader who recruits only people like himself or herself. There is another, better kind of leader who realizes you can only accomplish extraordinary things by involving excellent people who can do things that you cannot. Clinton surrounded himself with a critical mass of people with complementary virtues, often with talents very different from his own. Like most successful leaders, Clinton was unthreatened by his staffers, however competent, supremely confident that he had the vision that would win the race and that they had the skills. Unlike Ross Perot, who second-guessed and eventually dismissed his chief political strategist, Ed Rollins, Clinton constantly tapped the expertise of the team he had assembled. Like Walt Disney with *Snow White and the Seven Dwarfs,* Clinton carried the vision in his head. It was the staff's job to do each of the tasks necessary to make that vision a reality. As Clinton's chief political strategist, James Carville, recalls, Clinton told his staff he had the ideas necessary to win. "What I need most of all from you guys is focus, is clarity."

Several of Clinton's campaign staffers became celebrities in their own rights, notably the colorful Carville. But most of the members of Clinton's Great Group labored in obscurity, known only to the omnipresent media. For instance, one of Clinton's most important early moves was to raise a huge war chest. Clinton was initially burdened with a do-nothing fund-raiser, but quickly replaced him with a young whiz named Rahm Emanuel. Called Rahmbo at campaign headquarters because of his gung-ho style, Emanuel kick-started the campaign's fund-raising operation. Not a single Clinton fund-raiser had been scheduled during November 1991. With Emanuel in charge, twenty-seven money-raising events were held in December. By the end of 1991, the Clinton campaign had more than $3.3 million in the till, more than any other Democratic candidate had, giving Clinton a decided edge in the high-priced world of electronic campaigning.

There is no question that Clinton was the leader of the Great Group that effected his victory. But if the 1992 Clinton campaign had a star, it was not the candidate, but James Carville, the self-described Ragin' Cajun. Eccentric and outspoken, the Louisiana native was also a brilliant political strategist—the best in U.S. history, in the view of partner Paul Begala. Other people probably played equally important roles in the victory, including Begala and Clinton's soft-spoken director of communications, George Stephanopoulos. But Carville captured the public's imagination. And why not? Here was a man who looked, in the view of Fox News executive and Republican political consultant Roger Ailes, "like a fish who's swum too close to a nuclear reactor." Strange of visage, Carville was also single-minded of purpose. In Carville, Clinton got a True Believer in what Democratic politics could be and a political bulldog who would do anything, short of backing a racist or a Republican, to win.

Carville brought a street fighter's sensibility to the campaign. *All's Fair,* the joint memoir of the campaign Carville wrote with Republican rival, now his wife, Mary Matalin, opens with a quote that summarizes Carville's approach to politics: "When your opponent is drowning, throw the son of a bitch an anvil." Carville could be counted on not only to spin any controversy Clinton's way, but also to catch the media's attention. Reporters want good, colorful copy more than anything. Master of the striking Southern image, Carville had some of the same eccentric appeal for reporters as did Ross Perot.

Leaders of Great Groups find the right niche for each excellent contributor. The congenitally pugnacious

Carville ran what Hillary Rodham Clinton dubbed the War Room, which became the title of a documentary film about the campaign that won a 1993 Academy Award. The War Room was the nerve center of the campaign, Carville writes, and in many ways it was typical of the strictly functional quarters that Great Groups so often find for themselves. Located in commercial space in downtown Little Rock, the War Room was as isolated in its fashion as was Los Alamos.

Great Groups tend to be insular societies, cut off from big-city distractions. Carville liked the fact that there were no direct flights from Washington, D.C., to Little Rock. It made it that much harder for the Washington press corps to drop in and snoop. And if there was nothing much nearby to lure the War Room staff away from total immersion in a Clinton victory, that was fine with Carville, too. Carville expected his mostly young staff to work nonstop for Clinton's election. Winning was to be their vocation. Personally, Carville was so committed to the candidate that he put his long-term relationship with Matalin, deputy manager of Bush's reelection campaign, on hold for the duration. (The political odd couple spoke on the phone every morning and every night, but, they insist, only about what they were wearing and other noncampaign matters). Members of Great Groups are famous for having no lives outside the project. Who has time for real life, when you are making history?

In lieu of inviting decor, the War Room had the latest technology. Carville saw the campaign as a lightning war. The War Room responded to every attack on Clinton, every perceived threat, every opponent's stumble, and did so instantly. The War Room might be far

from the Beltway in miles, but it was linked, as completely as modern technology would allow, to the rest
of its own universe. That universe included Clinton
and his entourage on the road, the media covering the
campaign (referred to in the War Room as the Beast),
and the inner circles of the other primary candidates
and of Bush and Perot. No previous campaign so fully
exploited the achievements of computing's Great
Groups. The War Room was packed with computers,
fax machines, and other equipment that facilitated instant analysis and allowed the group to get information
or send it in a nanosecond. TV screens were everywhere. If the group had had a mantra, Carville suggests
in *All's Fair,* it would have been "This . . . is CNN,"
intoned by James Earl Jones. The all-news network was
on twenty-four hours a day.

"You create a campaign culture," Carville writes,
"and ours was based on speed." T-shirts were the uniform of this Great Group much of time, just as they
were of the Macintosh group. Carville favored one that
read, "Speed kills . . . Bush." If you were a grunt in
Carville's War Room, you ran to and from the copy
machine—you didn't walk. Like an actual military
campaign, the operation never slept. An overnight crew
tracked everything that Bush and his significant campaign others did and said and had briefing papers ready
for Carville and Stephanopoulos when they sat down
for their 7 A.M. meeting. Carville bossed and barked
and bullied in the best tradition of the sergeants he had
known in the marines. Nothing was to be done later
than now. Thus when Bush spelled out his economic
plan during the Republican convention in Houston,
the War Room dispatched briefing papers on why it

wouldn't work to the TV anchor booths before Bush finished the speech.

Many of Clinton's closest advisors were young. Stephanopoulos turned thirty-one as New Hampshire voters cast their primary ballots. Press liaison Dee Dee Myers was only twenty-nine. In actual years, Carville was one of the Great Group's elders: he was forty-eight when he signed on in 1991. But in demeanor, the Ragin' Cajun was decidedly adolescent. He dressed like a willful teenager, favoring jeans so tattered you could see his boxer shorts through them. He was capable of remarkable insights and obsessional focus, but he also had a childish tendency to get bored in meetings. The staff would provide him with toys to amuse himself with when his attention began to wander.

More than anyone else involved in the campaign, Carville was able to create the sense of high drama that characterizes so many Great Groups. Carville was aware that ad hoc organizations such as his need "rituals and moments" that become part of a common history. Intragroup rituals build cohesiveness, offer a welcome respite from long hours and high pressure, and imbue the enterprise with meaning. Carville established a tradition of recognizing the War Room employee of the week. The winner got a bottle of barbecue sauce and that most time-honored reward of childhood, a gold star. On one occasion, Carville decided that the best way to lessen the tension that had built up in the War Room was to crack eggs over a staffer's head.

Great Groups almost always have this quality of youthful brio. One reason may be that only the young or the somewhat deluded have both the energy and the inclination to spend it as profligately as these heroic efforts require. But there is more to it than that. Groups that change the world have an original vision, one that is as likely to be rooted in dreams as in experience. They see the world afresh, not necessarily the way others believe it to be. In a recent interview, Steve Jobs speaks of what is known in Zen as a "beginner's mind." Members of Great Groups often recall after their projects are over that they accomplished something remarkable because they didn't know they couldn't. Time and experience can undermine the godlike confidence—the creative chutzpah—that charges Great Groups. Jobs is a case in point. Now over forty, he no longer believes that technology will put a dent in the universe. "It's not as simple as you think when you're in your twenties—that technology's going to change the world. In some ways it will, in some ways it won't." It is not clear that today's more mature and reasonable Steve Jobs could have goaded the Macintosh team into greatness as the wild-eyed twenty-four-year-old did.

In many ways, every campaign is a Children's Crusade, a self-sacrificial effort on the part of thousands of volunteers willing to stuff envelopes until they drop. Carville was the head cheerleader of the Clinton campaign, its charismatic Mahdi, who could whip his soldiers into a frenzy and lead them into holy war. Carville had the charismatic leader's defining gift of being able to enlist others in his cause. He inevitably did so by casting Clinton's struggle for the presidency as a fight between Good and Evil, in which Clinton and his supporters were the virtuous underdogs.

Much of the energy of Great Groups seems to be generated by going up against a larger-than-life enemy. (In the electronics industry today, Microsoft's Bill Gates appears to be the Satan of choice). In *The War Room,* Carville is shown inspiring local volunteers on the eve of one of the crucial primaries. He rants against "the whole sleazy little cabal" of Republicans in power, from President Bush to Washington socialite Georgette Mosbacher. The speech doesn't quite scan word for word, especially in casting Mosbacher as the Devil Incarnate, but it rings emotionally true. Carville's is a passionate call to overthrow the status quo—to make sure that Georgette and all her overprivileged coconspirators are cut off forever from their fur coats and Lamborghinis. Carville has said he turns every campaign into a contest about class. Clinton's supporters were the noble little people, who would not only win this election but make the future safe from all the fat cats who would break the backs of ordinary citizens. Think about that "when your knuckles get tired and your feet get cold," Carville urges. "Don't forget who the real enemy is in here and don't forget who we are really campaigning against."

Finding the right message for Clinton was an essential element in his ultimate success. Carville believed the message had to be a simple one, and he knew what it should be. It hung on a sign in the War Room: "The economy, stupid." But equally important to the Clinton effort was the emphasis on change. As Clinton and his advisors realized long before Bush and his spinmeisters did, the American people had lost faith in government by 1991. "Change vs. more of the same" was another of the simple messages Carville had posted in the War Room. ("Don't forget health care" was the third.) In the demonology that Carville promulgated with such relish, Bush was yesterday. As shown in *The War Room,*

Carville once denounced Bush and his conservative politics with the sort of loathing usually reserved for child molesters. "He reeks of yesterday," Carville sneered. "The stench of yesterday. He is so yesterday if I think of yesterday I think of an old calendar with George Bush's face on it."

Carville's rhetoric is a reminder of just how powerful the underappreciated art of persuasion continues to be in collective action of all kinds. People are not necessarily swayed by reason. "The head has never beaten the gut in a political argument yet, and I doubt if it ever will," Carville writes in *All's Fair.* The Clinton staff developed a genius for tapping into the emotions and aspirations of a winning number of voters. That emotional appeal is not necessarily bad, although it obviously becomes so when put to evil use. But used responsibly, emotional resonance is the appeal of every speaker who is eloquent rather than simply articulate. Clinton campaigners found words and images that appealed to a deep-seated and widespread desire for change and for a renewal of hope. Within the group, charismatic individuals such as Carville were able to keep their staffs energized and focused by emotional appeals to campaign workers' desires to change the world and to defer personal interests to a worthy cause.

Great Groups coalesce around a genuine challenge, a problem perceived as worthy of a gifted person's best efforts. Much of the joy typical of Great Groups seems to reflect the profound pleasure humans take in solving difficult problems. The drive to problem-solve is as close to the heart of our species as is language—indeed, language itself may have evolved because of its utility in solving problems. Clinton's team was both driven by what it saw as a high purpose and sometimes giddy with the pleasure of outfoxing its opponents.

By the spring of 1992 it was clear that Clinton would get his party's nomination. He had pulled ahead of both saintly Paul Tsongas and otherworldly Jerry Brown, who remained a sour, chiding presence even during the Democratic convention. But it was not at all clear that Clinton could win the election. Perot, whose bid for the presidency was unexpectedly effective, forced Clinton to fight on a second front. Now he had both an incumbent opponent and a populist one who was making the change issue his own. Clinton also had two personal strikes against him as he went into the home stretch toward the July Democratic convention. First was the question of character that had been raised by Gennifer Flowers's detailed allegation that she had been his long-time lover (Flowers was the "smoking bimbo" Clinton's staff had long feared might surface). Later, Clinton's account of how he avoided military service during the war in Vietnam, which he opposed, exacerbated public doubts. Also looming over him was the widespread perception that he was just another politician. That perception could prove fatal in a contest whose hero of the moment was Perot, the billionaire underdog who stood for nothing so much as the end of politics as usual.

Clinton's staff knew their man had a huge problem to overcome, and they went about solving it in classic Great Group fashion—with imagination, with technological sophistication, with obsessional commitment, and, most important, collectively. Great Groups are contagious. They inspire other Great Groups. Thus Clinton media consultant Mandy Grunwald, once described as the Democrats' "Lee Atwater in a Chanel suit," came up with the perfect name for the top-secret operation to resurrect Clinton's candidacy. She called it the Manhattan Project. "Like the quest for the atom bomb for which it was named, it sought the means to victory in the arcana of science—in this case, the dimly understood complexities of opinion research rather than the knowable laws governing nuclear fission. And like the encampment of physicists, chemists, and engineers in the New Mexico desert half a century earlier, Clinton's strategists were racing against time," write the authors of *Quest for the Presidency 1992*. Like the people who made the bomb, the Clinton team understood that loose lips sink more than ships. The Manhattan Project was their insiders' name for the hush-hush project, officially given the attention-deflecting title the General Election Project.

The scientific side of this collaborative enterprise was the bailiwick of Stan Greenberg, an academic turned political consultant. Greenberg used focus groups and a related, more precise technique called dial groups to find out what people really thought of Clinton. The result was the unhappy discovery that focus-group participants thought of Clinton just as his political enemies had portrayed him, as "Slick Willie," an evasive man of less than unimpeachable character. One focus-group member complained, "If you asked his favorite color, he'd say, 'Plaid.' " The focus groups also confirmed what the team had long feared: many people thought of Clinton as a political insider and thus barely distinguishable from Bush. Greenberg wrote a memo summarizing the findings. Neither Gennifer Flowers nor the draft was Clinton's major problem, and nobody much cared whether he had inhaled. His biggest hurdle, Greenberg advised, was the belief that Bill Clinton is "the ultimate politician."

Now that the team knew exactly what people thought, they systematically tested what kinds of information improved Clinton's image. Often working with Grunwald, Greenberg found that telling dial group members a carefully edited version of Clinton's life history, emphasizing such appealing facts as his having been raised in a small town by a widowed mother, his confronting his abusive stepfather, and his refusal to use his office as governor to keep his brother out of prison on a drug charge greatly enhanced his appeal. Many were amazed to learn that Clinton was not a child of wealth, but a working-class kid. Many knew little or nothing about Clinton's personal history, including the fact that he and Hillary had a child, Chelsea. In the dial groups, which allowed people to register their degree of agreement or approval by turning up a dial, their displeasure by turning it down, Clinton's positive scores soared whenever his life was the subject. Greenberg and the others theorized that once Clinton was humanized and "depoliticized," voters would begin to hear his message.

Fine-tuning the message was also part of the Clinton Manhattan Project. In retrospect, it is evident that one of the reasons for Bush's defeat was that he never articulated a clear, positive, and compelling message. (It is not clear that any message could have overcome the presidency-ending image of a baffled Bush looking at a supermarket scanner as if it had just dropped from a distant planet. He might as well have muttered, "Let them eat cake.") Clinton's Great Group realized that the right message or messages would be critical to his winning the hearts and minds of the American voters. Carville's notion of a winning message is summed up in *Quest for the Presidency 1992*: "It had to be clear, it had to be real, it had to have a villain, and above all, in Carville's rules of war, it had to be optimistic."

Carville understood instinctively that leaders are purveyors of hope, not of despair. (Indeed, before Clinton and his wife went on *60 Minutes* to deal with the Flowers story, Carville wrote in the briefing memo, "Remember what Confucius said: 'A leader must be a dealer in hope.' ") Carville told his campaign colleagues: "We have to explain to people that something's wrong with the country, but in everything that Bill Clinton exudes, he smiles. He's an optimistic guy. People just have to sense we can turn this country around. We can get back on our feet. There is an answer." In Carville's schema, the villains were all the people, including Bush and Perot, who had made the system work for only a few. Clinton would make the country work for the people again. It was a simple, optimistic message (in *Leading Minds* Howard Gardner writes that successful political messages are pitched to the five-year-old mind). That Clinton happened to grow up in the small town of Hope, Arkansas, was almost too good to be true. He would brilliantly exploit that happy accident of history at the close of his acceptance speech at the 1992 Democratic convention when he told the cheering crowd, "I still believe in a place called Hope." Like the rest of the campaign process, the speech was a collaboration. The "place called Hope" line was from

Hillary Rodham Clinton, paraphrasing the script of a film about the Clintons made by TV producer and friend, Linda Bloodworth-Thomason.

Originality is a defining characteristic of Great Groups. Political image-burnishing usually involves avoiding risks, but Grunwald successfully argued that it was important to get the candidate onto the nontraditional media circuit to deliver his message. Clinton began appearing on TV shows no presidential candidate had ever considered doing before. On the *Arsenio Hall Show* he played "Heartbreak Hotel" on his sax. Earlier in the campaign, Clinton's handlers had nixed the gaudy ties he favored and put him in more dignified, more presidential neckwear. But for the hip, unconventional *Arsenio Hall* appearance, Dee Dee Myers and others cultivated Hall's wardrobe staff, who let them choose a flamboyant tie from Arsenio's private stash. Clinton worried that the Ray-Bans might be over the top, but decided to wear them anyway. As Carville liked to say, quoting Disraeli, "A good leader knows himself and the times."

Obsessive attention to detail is typical of Great Groups. Clinton's was as compulsive as any. Every TV spot and statement was vetted for nuance. Staff members took pleasure in making sure the product they were creating was perfect. Before the *60 Minutes* appearance, for instance, Grunwald reminded that Steve Kroft would be conducting the interview instead of Mike Wallace or one of the show's other veterans. Grunwald counseled that Kroft might try to establish himself as a big leaguer by asking tougher-than-normal questions. (The staff had not been able to get *60 Minutes* to agree to an unedited interview.) So Grunwald wisely suggested that the

Clintons might maximize their chances of getting particularly useful sound bites into the edited broadcast by saying "Steve" in the same breath and letting Kroft's ego work on their behalf.

A presidency is not made the way a bomb or a movie or a computer is made. But Clinton's successful run for the office was no less the work of a Great Group. The campaign had some of the same characteristics as the remarkable group effort that brought home the stranded astronauts of *Apollo 13*. As recounted by flight commander Jim Lovell in his book, *Lost Moon*, a mysterious in-flight explosion put the *Apollo 13*'s three-man crew in mortal danger for five days in 1970. The men were able to return safely to earth only because hundreds of people, including the astronauts and their NASA support team on the ground, were able to analyze and solve a series of complex technical problems— quickly, intelligently, calmly, and collaboratively. In Ron Howard's movie *Apollo 13*, based on Lovell's book, the scene in which NASA engineers figure out how to repair the spaceship's damaged air-cleaning system, using only materials on board, then talk the imperiled crew through the process of making the repairs, is absolutely thrilling—a powerful dramatization of the extraordinary achievement of a Great Group and of the exhilaration its members experience.

In the case of *Apollo 13*, three lives literally depended on the ability of the group to make and execute complex decisions quickly (the crew faced imminent suffocation, among other dangers). What is it about groups that allows them routinely to make better overall decisions than individuals do? We can speculate as to why: more options are thrown into the hopper, dead-end hypotheses are abandoned more quickly, another thinker may see a way to improve an idea he or she could not necessarily originate, intramural competition may spur the production of ideas, and the group may benefit from the fact that no one person has to bear all the responsibility for the results—a condition that is known to inhibit performance. (To paraphrase singer Tom Petty, sometimes it's good *not* to be king.) For all these reasons, groups are especially well adapted to solving complex problems in relatively short periods of time.

Great Groups tend to be less bureaucratic than ordinary ones. Terribly talented people often have little tolerance for less talented middle managers. Great Groups tend to be structured, not according to title, but according to role. The person who is best able to do some essential task does it. But Great Groups are rarely true democracies. They almost always have strong leaders. Someone must keep the project's music playing, must keep it on course. Clinton had an unusual and difficult role vis-à-vis his team in that one of his jobs was to make what fellow Southerner Dolly Parton calls "hurtin' decisions" that involved himself and his family. Clinton listened to what his advisors had to say even when he didn't want to hear it. As a result, he got good information, not just happy talk.

A presidential candidate is both an idea in the public mind and a real human being. Clinton's group was fortunate in its leader, despite his flaws. Clinton is a person who listens and learns. When he unexpectedly lost his second gubernatorial race in 1980, his response was to get in his car and travel the state of Arkansas, finding out why he had been thrown out of office. He not only listened to the harsh judgments of many of his former constituents, he did something much harder: he changed his behavior. He cut his hair, for instance, and he also stopped opposing the death penalty. When the Clintons learned that voters responded negatively to Hillary's using her maiden name, she chose to be called Mrs. Clinton at public gatherings.

During the 1992 campaign, Clinton accepted, albeit with difficulty, his strategists' advice that Hillary Rodham Clinton was perceived negatively and should become less visible for a time. Despite his reluctance to make public disclosures about private matters, Clinton also went along with the counsel that he tell his own story, including a certain amount about his violent stepfather. A person who loves to explore ideas in all their complexity, Clinton even accepted the wisdom of keeping campaign messages singular and simple.

Clinton made another major contribution to his own election by recruiting Al Gore to his Great Group. Clinton had considered everyone from Mario Cuomo to Bill Moyers and John Sculley as his running mate (Sculley was rejected when the staff learned that he had been married three times). But Clinton settled on Gore, the statesmanlike senator from Tennessee. Tapping Gore bucked the conventional wisdom that the vice presidential candidate should balance the ticket by being as unlike the presidential candidate as possible. Gore was a Southerner, close in age and values to Clinton himself. A fellow New Democrat, Gore shared the Clinton vision. But the choice of Gore did something far more important for the campaign. By choosing a running mate of the quality of Gore—a person who arguably would make a better president than Clinton himself—Clinton was widely perceived as too confident or principled to choose a second rater for the job. It was a brilliant move, and one that gave Clinton instant stature—presidential stature—in the minds of many previous doubters.

As a campaigner, Gore was notoriously stiff (he effectively mocked that quality throughout the 1996 campaign with jokes about his dancing the macarena). But Gore acquitted himself well in his televised debate with Bush running mate Dan Quayle and Ross Perot's second, the heroic, scholarly, but untelegenic Admiral James Stockdale. Bush's advisors had urged him to dump Quayle in '92, but Bush stuck with his vice president, despite Quayle's reputation as an extreme conservative with few intellectual gifts (comedians had a field day when Quayle publicly added a final *e* to the word *potato*). In the last analysis, it may have been the choice of Gore that tipped the election in Clinton's favor.

As a team, Clinton and Gore showed real rapport—another factor in the desired humanization of the candidate—during the innovative First Thousand Miles bus tour that marked the final weeks of the campaign. (Like every other aspect of the effort, the bus tour was a collaboration. The idea was proposed by campaign manager David Wilhelm. Throughout the campaign, the Clintons often relied on the counsel of their many media-savvy show-business friends and supporters. The bus tour was organized by one of them, Hollywood producer Mort Engelberg.) On the bus, Clinton, Gore, and their families went where no presidential-office seeker had gone for years—into what the *Quest* writers called "the heart of small-town America." People gathered by the thousands to see the man who promised to give the country back to them. Here was a prospective president who seemed as youthful as Kennedy had—a man who played hearts on the bus with his wife, who liked the music of Bonnie Raitt, and who not only hoisted babies, but didn't seem unduly distressed when they threw up on his expensive blue suits. For his part, Clinton seemed invigorated during the grueling last weeks of the fight by the very people who found hope in him. "You look at their faces," he said during the trek, "and they're allowing themselves to do something they haven't done for a long time: believe again."

In an interview, John Emerson, a White House staffer who ran Clinton's California campaigns in both 1992 and 1996, points out that if you focus too narrowly on *The War Room* and its stars, you overlook other major factors in Clinton's 1992 victory. According to Emerson, Clinton had first-rate operations in most of the states. The candidate, his War Room advisors, and the others who made up his national campaign team always determined the message of the day. But, Emerson says, it was up to the states to make sure the message was delivered effectively. Attempting to control the message, so the media was more or less forced to report on what the candidate wanted reported, was a lesson Clinton learned from the Republicans. "Reagan did this very well in 1984," Emerson says, but Clinton's run for office in 1992 "was the first Democratic campaign where the message was king."

Once the states knew the message of the day, they could reinforce it as they saw fit. Emerson recalls that California was able to exploit Dan Quayle's attack on

Murphy Brown, the sitcom TV personality and single mom played by Candice Bergen, by organizing pro–Murphy Brown parties throughout the state. Camera crews from *The Today Show* attended several, turning what could have been a successful Republican assault on liberal values into a plus for Clinton. "We were always looking for those kinds of opportunities," Emerson says. "The campaign was centralized, but it was also decentralized, and I think that was also part of the magic of it."

Emerson cites several other factors in Clinton's success in 1992 that have tended to be undervalued. One was the role of Mickey Kantor, who was national chairman of the campaign but was strictly a bit player in *The War Room*. In fact, Emerson says, Kantor made crucial contributions, including fund-raising. Kantor was also responsible for negotiating formats for the televised debates that favored Clinton. The most effective, Emerson says, was the debate that was "more like a *Phil Donahue Show*, where Bill Clinton could talk and George Bush was sitting there saying 'I don't get it' to the one woman and looking at his watch."

Emerson also cites the resource-allocation strategy developed by Eli Segal (campaign chief of staff) and David Wilhelm. "In the past, campaigns would buy national TV spots, so no matter where you lived, you saw the TV ad," Emerson explains. "This campaign bought regionally. So if we were fifteen points ahead in California, we didn't need to spend the additional marginal cost of having our TV spots aired in California. They should only air them in the states that were the true battleground states at that point. By the same token, if Texas was lost, why waste the time and money doing that?"

Finally, Emerson says, you can't underestimate the importance of what was happening on the candidate's press-packed plane. If the candidate "went off message" or handled some matter poorly, that became the story of the day, no matter what national headquarters had decided. The War Room was clearly "the focal point of the campaign," Emerson says, "but it was only one of about five significant components."

One of the attractions of a Great Group is its intensity. Carville and other members of the Clinton team speak of the almost sexual excitement of a presidential campaign. Campaign headquarters thrum with passion, fear, and other powerful emotions. Occasionally, there is actual sex as well, although rarely so much that it distracts the members from their grail-like goal. For the months of the campaign, the ordinary world seems very far away. (We will never know how many members of Great Groups remain in them as a way to avoid more traditional, less intense involvements and responsibilities, including caring for their children and interacting with their spouses.) When they look back, former members of Great Groups can typically recall the experience in minute detail and talk about it almost as if it had been a brief but wonderful love affair. "It was a summer romance," Tom West said of his leadership of the Data General computer project chronicled in *The Soul of a New Machine*. "But that's all right. Summer romances are some of the best things that ever happen." What happens in a Great Group is always in Technicolor. Life afterwards may seem as drab as a black-and-white movie.

Clinton's 1992 campaign resulted in the first Democratic presidency since that of Jimmy Carter and in a renewed, if not necessarily sustainable, national optimism. When Stephanopoulos looked back on the struggle, he remembered only its pleasures, not its constant tensions and sixteen-hour days. On the night of the victory, Stephanopoulos thanked Clinton and told him, "It was the best thing I ever did." Carville was moved to tears by Clinton's triumph and by the performance of his own crack young warriors. They had achieved something great, he told the members of his staff. "We changed the way campaigns are run," he said, before emotion overcame him. Ever eloquent in his down-home way, Carville finally found the perfect words to transubstantiate the protracted drudgery of the campaign into something glorious. "There's a simple doctrine," he said. "Outside of a person's love, the most sacred thing they can give is their labor."

Although Clinton's 1992 election was a historic triumph, as well as a superb example of creative collaboration, the first years of his presidency went less well. Much as fellow-Southern-governor-become-president Jimmy Carter had been, Clinton and many of the campaign staffers who followed him to the White House were perceived as Washington naifs, unskilled in its unique ways and insensitive to its time-honored rituals and prerogatives. The failure of Clinton's health-care-reform plan and other setbacks caused one Ivy League political scientist to characterize the first half of Clinton's first term as "two years of amateur hour." The Republican sweep of the congressional races in 1994 was widely perceived as a repudiation of the new president as well.

"Bill Clinton is the first president in history to have never had a honeymoon," says Emerson, in Clinton's defense. Republicans in Congress, used to having a lock on the White House, began attacking Clinton at once. Moreover, in Emerson's view, Clinton lacked the support of some lawmakers of his own party who may have simply envied his attaining the nation's highest office and of some who felt his positions were too moderate. A first-time president also needs some time on the job to master it, "to get your sea legs," Emerson says. It's a fair point. A study of hospital administrators found that it took individuals eighteen months before they felt comfortable in that far less demanding role. As Marshal Foch once observed, "It takes 18,000 casualties to make one general."

Emerson concedes that the new Clinton administration sometimes failed to communicate effectively. A major blunder, in his view, was miscalculating how the powerful Washington press corps would respond to its losing free access to certain areas of the White House. Emerson also believes Clinton was ill-advised to tackle the issue of gays in the military as the first item on his agenda (Emerson suggests that the Republicans led the media into pressing Clinton on the subject, which caused the new president to be seen as a "liberal in sheep's clothing").

Perhaps the problem was simply that Clinton, having raised expectations so high during the campaign, was less able in managing them once he was in office and had to deliver. Governing a nation is very different from winning an election. As former New York Governor Mario Cuomo once said, "Campaigning is poetry. Governing is prose." Governing not only requires very different skills, it may also require different personnel. The very people who thrive on the electricity of a War

Room may be ill equipped to handle the relentless routine that governing entails. Moreover, the intensity of a campaign may burn out those most involved in it.

In his 1996 reelection bid Clinton faced a very different challenge from the one he met so splendidly in 1992. As the incumbent, he could hardly call for sweeping change—to do so would be to repudiate his own administration. And he could no longer present himself as a political outsider. On the bright side, Clinton faced no opposition from within his party, making him the first candidate since FDR to enjoy that luxury. Moreover, the Republican candidates had thoroughly trashed each other before Bob Dole, a candidate with little charisma, emerged as the chosen. Dole entered the race with too little money and burdened both by fears that he, at 73, was too old for the office and by his association with Republican Speaker Newt Gingrich. He advanced his cause mightily, however, just as Clinton had in 1992, by his wise choice of a running mate. Dole tapped Jack Kemp, the popular, able, and vigorous former secretary of Housing and Urban Development. Long associated with supply-side economics, Kemp was able to reinforce Dole's major campaign theme of reducing taxes. A former National Football League quarterback, Kemp took to throwing footballs during his campaign appearances, causing one Dole staffer to observe that it was a good thing Kemp's sport hadn't been the javelin.

As the election approached, even the strengthening U.S. economy, in the words of a British journalist, seemed to be "rooting for Mr. Clinton." But, once again, Clinton was no shoo-in. The investigation into possible financial wrongdoing by the president or his wife in the Whitewater land deal refused to go away. In 1996, Clinton was determined to avoid the mistakes Bush had made as an incumbent candidate in 1992. ("It's the incumbency, stupid!" was a popular slogan among campaign insiders.) Unlike Bush, Clinton knew that a run for the presidency is never "just a two-month sprint." He began preparing for the campaign early. By .mid-1995 the president was meeting one evening a week in the family quarters of the White House to talk strategy with his top advisors. Throughout 1995 and into 1996, Clinton increasingly positioned himself as a centrist, albeit in a field shifted much to the right by conservative Republicans and their Contract with America. In the minds of some, Clinton moved too far right. Former speechwriter Paul Begala said so publicly and was shut out of the 1996 reelection effort.

According to Doyle McManus, chief of the Washington Bureau of the *Los Angeles Times,* Clinton went into the 1996 campaign not as a reformer, but as an accommodator. He declared in his 1996 State of the Union address that "the era of big government was over." Reversing his previous stance, he backed a balanced budget. In the months before the election, Clinton seemed to have arrogated much of the Republican agenda, including its emphasis on family values. Some supporters saw the president's shift away from issues such as health care to the rhetoric of the right as an act of political brilliance. Others saw the same positions, particularly his decision to cut federal programs for the poor, as a repudiation of the heart and soul of Democratic politics.

Despite the success of his 1992 team, Clinton assembled a very different group for 1996. George Stephanopoulos remained, but he failed in his effort to persuade the president to attack the Republican agenda as Harry S. Truman had in his 1948 "give 'em hell" campaign. Greenberg was no longer the chief pollster, reportedly because the president believed Greenberg had failed to prepare him for the Republican congressional rout of 1994. Greenberg was replaced by pollsters Mark Penn and Douglas Schoen. Henry Sheinkopf replaced Mandy Grunwald as media consultant and was replaced, in turn, by Bob Squier.

By the summer of 1996 the group of advisors gathering weekly in the Yellow Oval Room had grown to two dozen. The vice president was a key member of this campaign council, as were White House Chief of Staff Leon Panetta and Deputy Chief Harold Ickes. James Carville, who had been so prominent in 1992, did not attend. By far the most controversial advisor at these sessions was Dick Morris, an outside consultant who had started his political life as a Democrat but who had more recently advised Republican candidates.

Morris had helped make a much younger Clinton the comeback kid in the 1982 Arkansas gubernatorial race, when he won back the office he had lost in 1980. But Clinton and Morris had had a stormy relationship. Clinton had dismissed Morris more than once and was even said to have hauled off and slugged him on one occasion. But in the months before the Democratic convention, the president turned to Morris more and more regularly, to the dismay of Clinton's liberal advisors. Morris helped the president craft his new triangulation strategy, calculated to appeal to a broad spectrum of voters, including conservatives.

Even Morris's critics lauded his genius for turning polling data into effective political stands. But many observers were disturbed by his willingness to change parties. And some Clinton supporters, including White House insiders, were chagrined by charges that as recently as 1994, Morris had bad-mouthed both the president's policies and his character in the course of soliciting work from Republican candidates. Even worse in the view of some liberal Democrats was Morris's alleged willingness to do anything, including exploit racial tensions, to win elections, as Morris was said to have done when advising North Carolina Republican Senator Jesse Helms (Morris denied both allegations). One insider compared Morris to Rasputin.

Unlike the highly visible Carville, with his tattered jeans and memorable sound bites, the neatly suited Morris drew little attention to himself. He was a court politician, working inside, answering only to the president and perhaps to Mrs. Clinton. Morris's low profile, and his role in the campaign, ended abruptly August 29, 1996, as the president prepared to accept the Democratic nomination in Chicago. Morris resigned following allegations that he, a married man and the consultant responsible for the president's new family friendliness, had had a year-long affair with a prostitute. Most shocking was the charge that Morris had allowed her to eavesdrop on conversations with the White House. Morris neither confirmed nor denied the story, which had been pursued by the *Star*, a supermarket tabloid. Morris's resignation seemed to have no impact on

Clinton's speech that evening, in which he asked voters to allow him to be "the bridge to the twenty-first century," a phrase he repeated throughout the campaign. Morris immediately began putting the best possible spin on his predicament. A week after he resigned he announced a $2.5 million book deal.

Although Clinton's 1996 team triumphed, it had few of the characteristics—the energy, the sense of being winning underdogs, the disheveled but highly functional War Room, the youthful optimism, the belief that this was a collective enterprise that would change the world—that made Clinton's 1992 campaigners a classic Great Group. The kind of people who engage in creative collaboration want to do the *next* thing, not repeat the last one. Even before voters cast their ballots in 1996, media consultant Bob Squier and others had begun working on a fresh new project that promised the kind of original challenges no reelection campaign could. The task—getting Gore elected president in 2000.

THE SKUNK WORKS

It was an evil-smelling plastics factory next door that inspired the name of Lockheed's Skunk Works, a term that has become synonymous with secret, groundbreaking technological work.

In their autobiographies, both Skunk Works founder, Clarence L. "Kelly" Johnson, and his successor, Ben R. Rich, tell essentially the same story. Johnson was already a legendary designer of airplanes when, in 1943, he was asked to develop the first U.S. jet fighter to counter the formidable jets of the Luftwaffe. Arguing that it was the only way to get the job done and done quickly, Johnson persuaded his Lockheed bosses to let him create a top-secret department within the company, staffed by a small group of hand-picked engineers and mechanics. Kelly got the go-ahead to set up a hush-hush experimental operation that sidestepped the corporate bureaucracy and was beholden only to Lockheed's top management and its customers, notably the Army Air Corps. At the time, Lockheed's Burbank plant was filled to bursting with the workers and equipment required for around-the-clock production of military planes. But Johnson managed to find a bit of space next to the plant's wind tunnel for his elite cadre of twenty-three engineers, including himself, and thirty support people. They built their makeshift quarters out of wood from discarded engine boxes and roofed them with a rented circus tent. Their work was so secret they had neither janitors nor secretaries. Children whose fathers were in the Skunk Works grew up without ever learning exactly what Daddy did.

The name came from the funny papers. Politically savvy cartoonist Al Capp, the Garry Trudeau of his day, had recently created a character named Injun Joe for his popular comic strip, *Li'l Abner.* Injun Joe cooked up a particularly potent form of moonshine, called Kickapoo Joy Juice, from skunks, old shoes, and other unorthodox ingredients. The still was called the "Skonk Works." One day soon after Johnson's group was born, member Irv Culver answered the phone, "Skonk Works" (no secretaries, remember). The irascible Johnson, who had overheard, fired Culver for the offense, but the name stuck (and Culver continued to work in the Skonk Works he had named). Headed by thirty-three-year-old Johnson, that original Lockheed Skonk Works set out to design the first U.S. jet fighter in 180 days. Working furiously against its deadline, the group managed to produce a prototype of the P-80 Shooting Star with 37 days to spare. World War II ended before the plane could be produced in large numbers, but the P-80 was the U.S. fighter of choice in the Korean War.

Seventeen years after Johnson's people named themselves the Skonk Works, Capp's publisher balked at Lockheed's use of the term. In 1960, the group changed its name to the Skunk Works and registered both the name and its logo, a rakish skunk with an upturned nose. When Johnson died at the age of eighty in 1990, after a long decline that included the loss of his imposing mental powers, Lockheed ran a full-page memorial in its in-house magazine that read, "So long, Kelly," and showed the skunk with a tear running down its face.

Behind unmarked doors in Burbank, the Skunk Works produced some of the most remarkable planes ever conceived. Its revolutionary aircraft include America's first supersonic jet fighter, the F-104 Star-fighter, and the top secret U-2, the long-range reconnaissance plane that became known publicly only after the Soviet Union shot one down. Other remarkable planes to come out of the Skunk Works: the SR-71 Blackbird, a surveillance plane that flies at three times the speed of sound, and the F-117A, the stealth fighter-bomber best known for its role in the Persian Gulf War. (One of the pilots writes in Rich's book of the Baghdad raid, "We used to brag, 'Just tell us whether you want us to hit the men's room or the ladies' room and we'll oblige.' ")

Skunk Works creator Kelly Johnson was a visionary on at least two fronts—designing airplanes and organizing genius. Johnson seemed to know intuitively what talented people needed to do their best work, how to motivate them, and how to make sure that the desired product was created as quickly and as cheaply as possible. In time, Johnson wrote down the 14 rules under which his uniquely successful aeronautical lab operated. These included insights that should be cross-stitched on the sampler of every Great Group, such as giving near absolute control to the head of the group, limiting participation to a "small number of good people" (Johnson would have said "great people" in a less self-deprecating time), and keeping outsiders out. As the late Ben Rich noted shortly after he retired from the Skunk Works in 1991, "We had lived and died by 14 basic operating rules that Kelly had written forty years earlier, one night while half in the bag."

Johnson, who looked more than a little like W. C. Fields, was not a perfect leader. He had a terrible temper, and his staff was often scared to death of him. He became so impolitic as he grew older that some of his most important clients, including key air force decision makers, refused to deal with him. He eventually became a corporate liability as well as one of Lockheed's legendary strengths. But Johnson had certain characteristics that no leader of a Great Group is without. He loved excellence, and, as a result, he had an unerring eye for talent. And because he understood why talented people work, he was able to create an environment in which they thrived.

To be asked to join the Skunk Works was an honor. As former member H. S. "Blackie" Shanlian wrote to Tom Peters in 1984, Johnson wanted only the very best people for his team. Told he was the best to be had, each recruit tried to live up to Johnson's faith in him. When Tom West was putting together his Eagle computer team at Data General in the late 1970s, he took a similar approach. West and lieutenant Carl Alsing made it clear to potential recruits that only the best would be deemed good enough for the project. Instead of offering high salaries and other traditional inducements, the recruiters promised only two things—hard work and the chance to develop an exciting new computer that would "go as fast as a raped ape." "It was kind of like recruiting for a suicide mission," Alsing recalled. "You're gonna die, but you're gonna die in glory."

Once people were recruited to the Eagle project, they had to make a personal commitment to the enterprise, a rite of passage West called "signing up." This didn't involve actually signing anything like a contract.

Signing up, which takes place in almost all Great Groups, was a promise on the individual's part that he or she would do whatever it took to get the project completed successfully. Such pledges or vows, often unspoken, are almost never broken, because they are uncoerced, freely made by an individual who understands that the project will make extreme demands but has come to believe it worthy of his or her labor, time, and talent. It is no surprise that Great Groups will do almost anything to perfect their new technology or finish their movie. Not to do so would be to violate one's own integrity by breaking a promise made only to one's self.

Having been recruited by Kelly Johnson or Tom West amounted to public recognition of a person's excellence. Those selected were seen, by themselves as well as by others, as part of a creative elite, like Harvard Fellows or the winners of the so-called genius awards given by the John D. and Catherine T. MacArthur Foundation. Being part of an elite always implies obligations. Members of Great Groups tend to function with a sense of noblesse oblige, with the mind-set that much is expected of those who have received extraordinary gifts. This may be one reason that there is less conflict within Great Groups than within ordinary ones. (Being consumed by a project external to themselves is another reason for their relative tranquillity. Without such a project, collections of the talented can be as contentious as any group, as Black Mountain College proved again and again.) When people have a sure sense of their superiority, they tend to feel that the backbiting, jockeying for recognition, and general pettiness found in so many workplaces is simply beneath them. The fact that the other members of the group are excellent also encourages mutual respect.

The scientists at PARC, for instance, often disagreed heatedly at their weekly meetings, but they did so with the understanding that theirs were honest differences among peers in a distinguished scientific community. Moreover, they felt that these differences had to be aired in order to advance their common goal of discovering a new kind of computing. Properly deployed in such an atmosphere, debate can be a tool other than a wedge.

PARC's leader, Bob Taylor, had an especially deft way of resolving those conflicts that did surface. He employed a mediation model that eliminated the divisive win–lose element from arguments and substituted the goal of clarification. Taylor would urge people to move from what he called a Class 1 disagreement, in which neither party could describe the other's position, to a Class 2 disagreement, in which each side could articulate the other's stance. It may only have been Taylor's shrewd use of the principle of cognitive dissonance (the concept, dear to brainwashers, that you eventually come to believe whatever you say), but the technique usually worked. Taylor's mutually respectful model drained the heat from arguments and allowed the squabbling parties to find common ground. It's a rational technique, which allows the parties themselves to resolve conflicts in a mature, collegial way, that could be used in any group and hardly ever is.

Secrecy is one of the defining elements of what we have come to call a Skunk Works. At the original Skunk Works, born during World War II and in operation throughout the paranoid era of the Cold War, secrecy was seen as essential for national security. It wasn't until the Soviet Union toppled that the work of the Skunk Works was declassified, allowing Ben Rich to write about its achievements (in *Skunk Works,* cowritten by Leo Janos). It was a relief, Rich writes, to "stop playing mute, much like the star-crossed rabbi who hit a hole in one on the Sabbath." Occasionally, one of Johnson's or, later, Rich's hand-picked people had to be dropped from a project because security probes turned up some problematic associate or relative. At one point in the mid-1970s, when the Skunk Works was perfecting its revolutionary stealth technology, it had coffee cups made up that featured a cloud with the nose of the new plane coming out one end and a skunk's tail emerging from the other. The cups had to be locked up when not in use, lest someone without security clearance glimpse the classified design.

Whatever else that level of secrecy accomplishes, it heightens the *Mission: Impossible*-like excitement of whatever you are doing. The sense of being part of a uniquely informed cadre, privy to wonderful secrets from which the rest of the world is excluded, is also a powerful social glue. In the summer of 1955, for instance, only the team at the Skunk Works and a handful of others knew that the reason you couldn't find the bug spray Flit on store shelves was because it was being used to make a special low-vapor fuel for the highly classified new spy plane, the U-2. Many Great Groups are secretive even when they don't have to be. It's not surprising that West imposed a vow of silence on his group worthy of the Skunk Works or the Manhattan Project, forbidding them to use the name Eagle outside the group. At the computing company NeXT, founder

Steve Jobs insists on unusual openness within the group, but threatens that any leak to the outside world will bring an immediate end to internal candor.

Among Kelly Johnson's strengths was a sure grasp of what mattered to his people and what didn't. Most of them were engineers and tinkerers who hated paperwork, which he cut to an absolute minimum. Few reports were required (doubly wise, given the necessity of keeping track of and locking up classified documents). The exception—and one of Johnson's 14 famous rules—was that all important work had to be thoroughly documented.

Casual dress was another benefit of working for Johnson. In an era when no man went to the office in anything but full, blue-suited splendor, Johnson let his people work without suits and ties. The right to dress as one chooses is one of those perks that seems minor but has great resonance. Look how enthusiastically the U.S. workplace has adopted "casual Fridays." The necktie is not as humiliating a symbol of the loss of personal freedom as is the uniform with first name embroidered above the pocket. But every American worker knows that a dress code is a form of social control, an unpleasant reminder that the boss can not only tell you what to do, but he or she can also tell you what to wear, just as Mommy and Daddy used to do. Allowing workers to dress as they please instantly increases collegiality. Great Groups may create their own uniforms—sandals at Black Mountain, T-shirts for makers of the Macintosh. In those cases, clothes help make the team. But talented, independent thinkers always prefer to dress themselves. As people of unusual imagination, they may choose to dress creatively, if they bother to think about the matter at all.

Great Groups work murderous hours, often with deadlines that cause stress levels to soar. Reducing stress, rather than adding to it, is one of the functions the leader must often perform. Even during World War II, when their groups were working frantically, both Oppenheimer and Johnson insisted that their staffs take Sundays off.

Great Groups work as if possessed. But they also always manage to have fun. Johnson made it a point to invite all the mechanics as well as the engineers to observe the initial flights of new Skunk Works planes. Then they partied. After the first U-2 flight, Johnson recalls in his 1985 autobiography, "all of us celebrated with the usual beer and arm-wrestling contests." Johnson, who had pumped up as a teenager doing construction work, often won, and not just because he was the boss.

Tapped by Johnson in 1954, Rich remembered his years as a member of the Skunk Works as both fulfilling and full of adolescent high spirits. "Working to giddiness, we acted like college sophomores a shocking amount of the time," he writes. The boys decorated their walls with pinups that could be turned over to show more socially acceptable pictures of ducks whenever their quarters were visited by bigwigs from the Central Intelligence Agency or other Skunk Works clients. Rich acquired the nickname Broad Butt as a result of winning a spontaneous contest among the lads to see who had the largest posterior. Ever the engineers, they used calipers to make their measurements. After Rich was picked by Johnson to succeed him in 1975, Rich adopted the decidedly juvenile name Ben Dover to use as cover when traveling on top-secret business.

Some of this playfulness reflects the reality that problem solving is pleasurable. People engaged in successful collaborations are getting an immediate payoff in increased endorphin production, comparable to a runner's high or the sense of well-being that follows good sex. No wonder Great Groups engage in water fights, drink copious amounts of beer, and arm wrestle. They feel good.

Much of the communication within Great Groups is nonverbal. Members understand the shared vision so profoundly that they often don't need language to communicate. But, while members of Great Groups may be able to work together on some problem without saying much of anything, such groups typically develop a language of their own. Like the private language of twins, this groupspeak allows them to exclude the uninitiated and to declare their collective identity.

Johnson's people at Lockheed developed their own names for things, starting with the term *Skunk Works* itself. Following Johnson's lead, the group referred to President Eisenhower, whom Johnson thought indecisive, as Speedy Gonzales. In Tom West's group at Data General, the insiders' language of computer hackers mutated into an even more private form of Eaglespeak. People working on the Eagle project expressed the fear that their computer would not be a real advance on the company's existing model. They didn't want to "build a bag on the side of the Eclipse." West says that he thinks the creation of a subculture, with its own language, is not just typical of Great Groups, but predictive of their ultimate success. "I think you can almost identify projects that are going to be successful by the fact that they have invented their own world. If you wanted to find a litmus test for whether this stuff is working or not, it would be whether they invented their own language."

In organizing his Skunk Works, Johnson paid no attention to how the quarters looked or how comfortable they were. One of the principles he held dearest was that designers and mechanics should work side by side, making suggestions and addressing problems as they went along, so the prototype could be modified on the spot. In the Skunk Works, desks were crammed together, prompting one engineer to post a sign that read, "Privacy sucks." No one seemed to mind, perhaps because their concentration on the task counteracted what in less-intense groups can be the hell of other people. Rich remembered his early colleagues as "all young and high-spirited, who thought nothing of working out of a phone booth, if necessary, as long as they were designing and building airplanes." He writes that he learned to love the "slumlike conditions," even the ubiquitous cigarette smoke.

The tendency of great things to be accomplished in dreadful spaces should give architects and decorators pause. There is something about the controlled chaos of a garage, the joyless interior of a Quonset hut, that seems to spur the imagination. Perhaps the charmlessness of these places forces the people who work in them to turn inward, where problem solving takes place. Certainly these environments offer few distractions, including comfort. For reasons still to be discovered, creative collaboration seems to be negatively correlated with the plushness of the office or the majesty of the view. Awful places have come to be seen as almost a requisite for a Great Group. James E. Moxley, president of Ultra Technologies, remembers with fondness the bleak quarters in which his company started up. "It was an extremely good spot for incubating a business," he recalls of the space in which his subsidiary of Eastman Kodak did innovative work involving lithium batteries. "The atmosphere was *right*. The place had little heat, no air-conditioning, no screens, no carpeting and bare light bulbs." For a group that was inventing itself, it was just about perfect.

People wanted to work at the Skunk Works not because it was plush or prestigious, but because they loved the work. People in Great Groups would do what they do even if they didn't get paid for it. And what they inevitably do is sustained problem solving.

One of the ways Johnson made his reputation was by delivering radically new planes on time and under budget. To do so, he routinely incorporated existing parts, available right off the shelf, into the new designs. (Using existing parts lowers costs and speeds up design and production. It also means that the evolving plane will include at least some parts that are known quantities in terms of durability and the like.) But the SR-71, the Blackbird, which the group began designing in 1958, presented a whole new order of challenge. According to Johnson, the Blackbird was "the toughest job the Skunk Works ever had." The plane had to be capable of things no plane had achieved before—or has since, for that matter. It had to fly at three times the speed of sound or better, at altitudes above 80,000 feet. It also had to be hard to detect by radar and capable of global flight, which meant in-flight refuelings. Flying so high and so fast, every bolt and system of the plane would be exposed to unprecedented heat and other stresses. The streamlining techniques, including cannibalization of parts from other models, that had worked so well for Johnson in the past had to be abandoned for the Blackbird.

"Everything about the aircraft had to be invented," Johnson writes. "Everything." That meant structural materials, manufacturing techniques, fuels, and paints, not to mention the revolutionary design. Given the ironic code name Oxcart, the plane was the first to be built from titanium. Lockheed obtained much of the rare material in the Soviet Union, through CIA fronts. Every aspect of the design and construction of the plane presented a long string of problems that its creators solved with gleeful ingenuity. (Although the intellectual work was fun, it was deadly serious as well. Everyone knew that a miscalculation could mean the death of a pilot.) To make the plane less visible to radar and still get sufficient aerodynamic lift, chines, or ridges, were added to the fuselage. "The result, head on, looks like a snake swallowing three mice," Johnson writes. Fabrication presented the plane's creators with as many puzzles to solve as had the design. For instance, spot welds on the wing panels sometimes failed when the planes were built in the summer, but not at other times of the year. After scrutinizing the entire process, the staff discovered that the Burbank water system was to blame. In the summer, large amounts of chlorine were added to the water to suppress the growth of algae, and the chlorine compromised the welds. The problem disappeared when the welds were rinsed with nonchlorinated water.

The Blackbird, introduced in 1964 and retired in 1990, was the antithesis of a lumbering, earthbound oxcart. It was capable of flying 2,092 miles an hour at 85,068 feet. It once flew from Los Angeles to Washington, D.C., in 64 minutes.

The visceral pleasure of solving tough flight-related problems was one Johnson continued to seek in his retirement. In his autobiography, he writes that he often entertained himself while doing laps in his pool by asking, "How would I make an airplane from scratch?"

One of Johnson's great strengths as a leader was his ability to distinguish between excellence and perfection. The Skunk Works, Disney Animation, and the Macintosh team were remarkably innovative, but they weren't think tanks—institutions whose real mission is the production of ideas. These Great Groups were places where products were being made, things that had to be delivered in a timely fashion to the world. One of Steve Jobs's mantras at Apple was "Real artists ship." Johnson, too, believed that a plane must be designed brilliantly but not so perfectly that it never gets off the drawing board. In Johnson's view, some things, notably safety, must never be compromised. He built triple redundancy into the Blackbird, for instance, so that a failure in any one system, or even two, would not mean the loss of a pilot. But, like Thomas Aquinas before him and Steve Jobs after, Johnson knew that something that exists is intrinsically better than something, however brilliantly conceived, that doesn't. Real engineers ship. Rich, who headed the team that designed the Blackbird's air-inlet control system, recalled that it took six months to design a system that was 70 percent efficient, but another fourteen months to boost its efficiency to 80 percent (the system was largely responsible for the plane's unprecedented propulsion). When the system achieved 84 percent efficiency, Johnson decided enough was enough, just as Roy Disney had in ruling that the Prince in *Snow White* would just have to shimmy.

"We aimed to achieve a Chevrolet's functional reliability rather than a Mercedes' supposed perfection," Rich writes. "Eighty percent efficiency would get the job done, so why strain resources and bust deadlines to achieve that extra 20 percent." Protected by their leaders from the distracting exigencies of real life and high on the feel-good brain chemicals of discovery, members of Great Groups can become obsessed with the process and reluctant to commit to an imperfect solution, however wonderful it may be. One of the leader's critical tasks is to let the members hear the siren song of perfection without abandoning the goal of delivery. Like politics, successful collaboration is the science of the possible.

At the Skunk Works, Johnson made it clear that he, not one of his subordinates, would be the person who donned suit and tie and interacted with Washington honchos. Johnson had an especially close relationship with the CIA's Richard Bissell, who was Allen Dulles's special assistant and liaison with the Skunk Works until pulled off the job in 1959 to organize the ill-fated Bay of Pigs invasion. Rich describes Bissell as an advocate for the Skunk Works within the government. "Bissell was godfather to the Skunk Works," Rich writes. "He started the U-2 and that really put us in business to stay."

That Lockheed was engaged in what amounted to the creation of a secret air force for the CIA may make you uneasy. But, however disturbing the politics that surrounded it, the U-2 was a technological wonder. The spy plane was originally proposed to Eisenhower by Edwin Land, creator of the Polaroid technology, who was developing the project's high-resolution camera. A super lens was being developed by Harvard astronomer Jim Baker. And the secret mandate given to Lockheed in 1953 was to design a plane that could fly over the Soviet Union at more than 70,000 feet, preferably without being detected, and take surveillance photos unprecedented in their clarity. The Skunk Works' job was to design and build a plane that would fly so high that no telltale vapor trail would be visible from the ground, that would have a range of more than 4,000 miles, and that would be sufficiently steady that its surveillance photos would not be blurred.

When test pilot Tony LeVier was first shown a blueprint of the resulting U-2, he described it as "a big goddam sailplane with the longest wingspan I ever saw—like a goddam bridge." The plane had a wingspan of eighty feet and broke all records for altitude and range. Essentially a platform for its remarkable cameras, the U-2 began flying over the Soviet Union in 1955, at a time when U.S. schoolchildren were being drilled in ducking under their desks and covering their heads in case of a nuclear attack by the Soviets. For almost five years, the overflights provided the CIA and U.S. military with detailed pictures of Soviet military installations, including its proliferating missile bases, and other invaluable intelligence. According to former CIA director Richard Helms, building the U-2 was the agency's smartest decision, "the greatest triumph of the Cold War."

The U-2 was the result of creative collaboration among dozens of brilliant people under Johnson's gruff leadership. Everything from the condorlike shape of the aircraft to its superlight aluminum fuselage was an innovation. When new problems arose during the design, testing, and manufacturing process, as they did daily, imaginative solutions were found. In flight, for instance, the engine tended to spray oil on the windshield of the cockpit. A mechanic came up with a decidedly nontraditional fix—packing sanitary napkins around the oil filter to absorb the oil before it could splatter.

One problem the group couldn't solve was that Soviet radar had little or no trouble tracking the planes. For several years, the Soviets had no weapon that could reach the high-flying giants, but they knew immediately when one was flying over. In an effort to limit what the U-2 cameras could see, the Soviets flew formations beneath the spy plane, a maneuver that Johnson referred to as "aluminum clouds." But in 1960 the inevitable happened. A U-2, piloted by Francis Gary Powers and flying ten miles above the Soviet Union, was brought down by a ground-to-air missile. (Johnson suspected that an electronic black box in the tail of Powers's U-2, designed to confuse the Soviet missiles, had actually helped them home in on the aircraft.) Powers chose not to use the needle of poison he had been equipped with and was captured, to Khrushchev's delight. The incident greatly embarrassed Eisenhower, who had long claimed that the U-2 was not a spy plane, but simply an airborne lab for gathering meteorological data. The flights over the Soviet Union were halted, and Powers, put on display in Moscow, was tried and found guilty of espionage. But a new use for the U-2 was quickly found—overflying the People's Republic of China. In the 1990s the plane, which is still operational, was used to gather intelligence on Iraq.

Kelly Johnson and Ben Rich had markedly different leadership styles. A CIA official who worked with both said, "Kelly ruled by his bad temper. Ben Rich rules with those damned bad jokes." Johnson liked to say that his philosophy of management was "to lead people, not to drive them." But, in fact, he was often a bully. He was also one of the greatest aircraft designers of all time. If the people who worked for him had to endure his bursts of temper and other character flaws, they also knew that the remarkable planes they created would never have existed without him. Much as Disney did, Johnson had the kind of genius that goes far in making up for flawed "people skills." Rich observed, "In the mere act of trying to please him and live up to his expectations, I became twice the man I otherwise would have been."

But the people who worked for Johnson could depend on him for more than setting a daunting standard. He did everything he could to protect his group from the meddling of corporate "suits," the bean counters and go-by-the-book types who can so easily undermine a creative enterprise by trying to tame it and bring it under corporate control. (Not the least of Johnson's accomplishments in this department was the creation of the Skunk Works itself.) Johnson told Rich that one of the undervalued virtues of tight security was that it kept the corporate types at bay. At the same time that Johnson was protective of his people, he had a realistic understanding of the need to represent the Skunk Works' interests within the company. He sought and obtained a seat on the board of directors in order to do so more effectively. Great Groups need to know that the person at the top will fight like a tiger for them. It was one of the things that the PARC group admired most about Bob Taylor. Interestingly, Tom West fought hard for his Eagle group at Data General but chose not to tell them, reasoning that it would only distract them from the project. As a result, some of his team wondered what he did all day. That decision caused almost as much unhappiness as West's failure to say hello to members of the group.

At the Skunk Works, Johnson's people could also depend on his absolute integrity. He categorically refused to build a plane he didn't believe in, even if it meant Lockheed's losing money on the deal. He returned millions of dollars to the air force after he became convinced that even his team couldn't build a hydrogen-powered plane. He also demonstrated his integrity in getting Gary Powers a job as a U-2 flight-test engineer when the pilot, thought by many Americans to be a traitor, returned after two years in a Soviet prison. Johnson said he believed five things "were really important in life." They included belief in God, good health, a sense of purpose, and a loving and understanding spouse. The fifth was the "respect of the people for whom you work and who work for you." The people who worked for Johnson may not have liked him very much, but they had every reason to respect him. Some talented people are obviously able to work for individuals whose integrity is compromised, even people who are evil (physics giant Werner Heisenberg was willing to build an atomic bomb for Hitler). But most talented people have little incentive to defer to an individual without a strong moral core. Genius, even simple excellence, multiplies personal options. Why follow someone you can't trust or who makes you feel soiled?

Johnson's command-and-control leadership style was that of his generation, one that respected authority and expected subordinates to respect it as well. Johnson didn't feel obliged to explain his actions to his team members, he didn't share his authority, and he didn't care if his team liked him or not, as long as it respected him. The Skunk Works was born during World War II, a time when you were expected to do whatever your leaders told you to do, without hesitation. Johnson's group was far more collegial than many, but it was no participatory democracy. At this point in time, it is impossible to know if Johnson's authoritarian leadership style began to drive people away from the Skunk Works. However abrasive, he continued to design revolutionary planes, and he had become a genuine legend, the person who showed Amelia Earhart how to maximize her mileage on her ill-fated 1937 flight around the world, the person who once took the controls away from Howard Hughes when he decided Hughes wasn't flying safely.

But times were changing, and a different kind of leader was called for. Johnson strongly recommended Ben Rich to succeed him. You wonder if Johnson did not take the same methodical but creative approach to solving the problem of his successor as he did to designing an airplane. He certainly knew how different Rich's style was from his own. In contrast to the crusty Johnson, who spent little time chatting up his employees, Rich was a self-styled schmoozer. He constantly told jokes, supplied to him by his brother, producer of a

TV sitcom. Rich was "user-friendly," in his own description. He was decisive, he could chew people out, but he also believed that good morale was important and that the well-placed compliment was an invaluable management tool. To polish his leadership ability, Rich had taken a thirteen-week course in advanced management at the Harvard Business School in 1969. Johnson mocked Rich for it and told him he wouldn't learn anything at Harvard that he couldn't learn observing Johnson in the Skunk Works. But Johnson may have sensed that he was becoming an anachronism and that a new era of professional management was at hand. Whatever reservations Johnson had, he wrote the enthusiastic recommendation that Rich believed got him into the Harvard program. Johnson had no intention of changing the way he ran the place, but, when he had to retire at sixty-five, he turned his beloved Skunk Works over to a leader who managed greatness with a much lighter touch than Johnson's own.

Rich, who died of cancer of the esophagus in 1995 at the age of sixty-nine, was a talented engineer, but he lacked Johnson's aviation genius. Like so many other leaders of Great Groups, Rich was creative by orchestrating the creativity of others. For the most part, he let his technical people make their own informed judgments. One of Rich's program directors described him as "the perfect manager." Rich's contribution was "to let us do our own thing and smooth our way with the Air Force and Lockheed management. . . . He would defend and protect us if we screwed up and keep us viable by getting new projects and more money."

During Rich's tenure, the Skunk Works developed the stealth technology that revolutionized the way modern war is waged. For years, the Skunk Works had been devising ways to make its military aircraft less visible to enemy radar by altering the shape of the plane and using materials that absorb radar (the Blackbird had unprecedented stealthiness for its day). Rich had been in charge of the Skunk Works for only about six months when one of his radar specialists, thirty-six-year-old Denys Overholser, presented Rich with what he later called "the Rosetta Stone breakthrough for stealth technology."

As Rich tells in *Skunk Works,* the key was an article written by a Soviet radar scientist almost a decade before, which had just been translated into English. As Overholser explained to Rich, the paper by Pyotr Ufimtsev (who joined the UCLA faculty in 1990) described a method for calculating precisely how much electromagnetic radiation would be reflected by a given geometric shape. (To determine the size and location of an object, radar sends out an electromagnetic beam and then analyzes the electromagnetic energy reflected back.) Using the equations in the article, Overholser believed he could write computer software that would calculate in advance exactly how visible to radar planes of different designs would be. The computer technology of the period was only powerful enough to do the calculations in two dimensions. But Overholser didn't think that was an insurmountable problem. He proposed designing a plane consisting entirely of flat triangles. Rich recognized the value of the work at once. He decided that the Skunk Works would go ahead and design the first all but undetectable plane, however odd it looked.

Rich gave Overholser three months to write the software. In best Skunk Works fashion, he collaborated with his retired octogenarian mentor, Bill Schroeder, and did the job in five weeks. While Rich sold Lockheed on the project and talked his way into a Defense Department's Advanced Research Projects Agency competition for a new stealth fighter, Overholser used his computer to design an aircraft that would barely register on a radar screen. The result, Rich recalled, was a plane that looked like "a diamond beveled in four directions." Overholser dubbed it the Hopeless Diamond.

As Rich recounts in *Skunk Works,* he pressed Overholser on just how small the plane's radar signature would be. The new plane would be one thousand times less visible than the stealthiest previous design, Overholser assured him. That would look how big on a radar screen? "As big as an eagle's *eyeball,*" Overholser answered. Rich gave Overholser full credit for finding the key to unprecedented stealthiness. But Rich did boast of one contribution that he made to the development of the bizarre-looking plane. Rich had the inspired idea for selling the design at the Pentagon. "Here's the observability of your airplane on radar," he would say as he rolled a ball bearing across the table.

The Skunk Works had always developed its new planes in a highly collaborative manner, taking good ideas from anyone involved in the process, from engineers to test pilots. A new, all-but-invisible stealth fighter was no exception. As always happens, challenges occurred at every turn, from the design of the tail pipe to a shortage of skilled aerospace workers who could pass the drug test (44 percent of the applicants failed). The shape of the plane is the better part of stealth, but low observability also results from special coatings and other materials. Parts of the new plane were coated with a special radar-absorbing paint. During testing, the paint suddenly began to fail. The team's problem busters simply couldn't find the source of the problem. Then, a member spoke to someone at DuPont, which was supplying the paint, and discovered that DuPont had changed the formula without telling the Skunk Works. Later, during the manufacturing phase of the project, there was a dramatic increase in foreign-object damage, or FOD. This happens when a worker accidentally leaves a screw or other object in an engine or when objects fall out of pockets and are left behind. One creative solution: workers were issued coveralls without pockets.

Six years after Overholser had given Rich his Rosetta stone, the new plane, now called the F-117A stealth fighter, was in the sky. The F-117A was so stealthy that the hangars in which the planes were stored would sometimes be littered with the battered little bodies of bats that had crashed into the planes when their echolocation systems failed to sense their presence. The F-117A showed what it could do on the first night of Desert Storm, described by military historian John Keegan as "the most complex air-ground-sea campaign in the history of warfare." The stealth planes flew over Baghdad undetected until they began knocking out Iraqi communications and other targets with amazing accuracy while the world watched on CNN. According to Rich, the F-117A fighter-bombers made up only 2 percent of the allied air force, but they were responsible for 40 percent of all the targets hit. Not a single stealth pilot was lost in the brief war. Rich, who was at a retirement banquet when Desert Storm began, recalls proudly in his book, "the only way the enemy knew the

F–117A was in the sky above was when everything around him began blowing up."

However fierce his rhetoric, Rich brought a kinder, gentler leadership style to the Skunk Works. He was able to work with the Pentagon personnel whom Johnson had alienated. Rich may have lived by Johnson's 14 rules, but he had some of his own insights into what made the Skunk Works so effective. He believed, for instance, in the value of generalists "who are more open to nonconventional approaches than narrow specialists." (Both the Manhattan Project and Xerox PARC similarly benefited from the presence of people who were not narrow specialists, but deep generalists.) Rich once summed up what the Skunk Works was all about this way: "We encouraged our people to work imaginatively, to improvise and try unconventional approaches to problem solving, and then got out of their way."

Great Groups are places where you have the opportunity to see just how good you are. The project is challenging enough to test your limits. The others in the group are stimulating and worthy of respect. Rich recalled of his early years at the Skunk Works, "Each day I found myself stretching on tiptoes to keep pace with my colleagues." The experience was "invigorating and fun." It was also an opportunity to soar.

EXPERIMENT AT
BLACK MOUNTAIN

The end of Black Mountain College, the legendary experimental school in the foothills of western North Carolina, was tragicomic. As Martin Duberman writes in his pioneering 1972 history of the school, Black Mountain became so impoverished toward the end that some faculty and students shoplifted food from the A&P in town, secreting steaks inside oversized trousers. By 1954–55 the college was so strapped that it decided, after much anguished discussion, to admit the retarded son of a wealthy man in hopes of extracting a substantial gift from him. Poet Robert Creeley, who was then on the faculty, remembered that the father was to fly over the campus and waggle the wings of his plane if the crazy plan were a go. Creeley told Duberman, "And so for a period of at least three or four days, we were wandering around in various fields adjacent, staring up to the sky and listening for the sound of this plane, which never came. . . . I don't think I've ever seen more extraordinarily gifted men put to such an extraordinarily absurd task."

Black Mountain College finally closed, after twenty-three remarkable years, in 1956. It was never accredited (although its students were routinely accepted at Harvard and other prestigious institutions). It rarely enrolled more than 100 students a year. It was chronically underfunded, as a result of which faculty often went unpaid. It had virtually no library except the books brought to it by its faculty and students. And yet no college in U.S. history has had a greater impact on the arts than did Black Mountain. The list of greatly talented people associated with the school includes such luminaries as artists Willem de Kooning, Franz Kline, Josef Albers, Robert Motherwell, Robert Rauschenberg, Cy Twombly, Ben Shahn, and Jacob Lawrence; architects Walter Gropius and Marcel Breuer; poets Creeley, Jonathan Williams, and Charles Olson, novelists James Leo Herlihy and Francine du Plessix Gray; critics Eric Bentley and Alfred Kazin; composer John Cage; dancer-choreographers Merce Cunningham and Agnes de Mille; director Arthur Penn; and visionary Buckminster Fuller. Black Mountain was the site of John Cage's first multimedia "happening" and the place where Fuller erected his first geodesic dome. Merce Cunningham founded his dance troupe at Black Mountain. And it was the home of *The Black Mountain Review,* whose final issue in 1957 was a preview of what was coming next in American literature. That single volume included Allen Ginsberg's poem "America," a story by Jack Kerouac, and sections from two as yet unpublished novels, William Burroughs's *Naked Lunch* and Hubert Selby, Jr.'s *Last Exit to Brooklyn.*

Throughout its twenty-three years, Black Mountain was both college and community, a place that drew extraordinary people and brought them into relentless, sometimes bruising contact with each other, far from the distracting options of urban life. It was, as Martin Duberman writes, "an occasional loony bin, a rest camp, a pressure cooker, a refuge, and a welfare agency," but, above all, it was a place where people, whether they were officially faculty or students, learned life-changing lessons from each other.

In 1945, Black Mountain became the first nonblack college in the modern South to enroll African-American students. And although it can hardly be said to have established the current pattern of higher education in the United States, it was, for a time, the world's most exciting laboratory for the testing of such forward-looking ideas as the blurring of the boundaries between learning and the rest of life, recognition of the value of physical labor as an educational experience, and the elimination of traditional course requirements and grades. Such innovative schools as the University of California at Santa Cruz are surely the heirs of Black Mountain, and Black Mountain played a seminal role in the creation of the T-group, or encounter group, sensitivity training, and the Human Potential Movement. Moreover, you can't help wondering if such now widely accepted pedagogical ideas as learning as a life-time process would have taken hold if Black Mountain had never existed.

Above all, Black Mountain was a Great Group, one that managed, much as Disney Feature Animation has, to reinvent itself. In its twenty-three years it had three extraordinary leaders, beginning with founder John Andrew Rice. A graduate of Tulane University and a Rhodes scholar, Rice was a charismatic and creative teacher in an era when uninterrupted lectures were the classroom norm. Rice delighted in prodding his students into questioning their beliefs and received notions, so much so that one of his students insisted that Socrates must have looked like Rice. At Rollins College in Winter Park, Florida, where Rice was a professor of classics in the early 1930s, he was always willing to depart from the expected curriculum to take the educational process wherever the students led it.

Like so many Great Groups, including Steve Jobs's digital pirates, Black Mountain defined itself by its opposition to the conventional. Black Mountain would never have existed if Rice hadn't been fired in April 1933 from his teaching post at Rollins. A progressive institution in many ways, Rollins was run autocratically by its president, Hamilton Holt. Rice's offense was to have served on the college committee that recommended the abolition of Rollins's unique eight-hour day, an innovation of Holt's that divided the student's day into four two-hour classes. Less than a week after Rice and the rest of the curriculum committee made its recommendation, Rice was asked to resign. When he refused, he was dismissed. He subsequently infuriated Holt by appealing the dismissal to the American Association of University Professors. Among the hodgepodge of bizarre charges Holt read against Rice at the subsequent AAUP hearing were that he appeared on the beach in a jockstrap, he had a lazy walk, he had caused a rift between a female student and her sorority, and he had hung obscene pictures in his classroom. By the end of the school year, eight faculty who had sided with Rice had either been fired or had resigned. The editor of the school paper and a number of other students decided to quit Rollins as well. Six months later, the official AAUP report would side with Rice and against Holt, but, by that time, Rice and his band of campus rebels were already in the Carolina foothills, making history.

Since it was the height of the Depression, Rice and his jobless supporters were unlikely to find teaching posts at other established schools. So, Rice proposed that the group start a college of their own, one that would reflect their own view of what learning was about. Theirs was indeed a dream with a deadline. The plan was to open the doors of the college that fall. In that busy summer of 1933, Rice and his fellow academic utopians accomplished an enormous amount. The school was incorporated, Rice obtained commitments from the eleven other men and women who would serve with him on the faculty, and they rustled up twenty-two students, most of them from Rollins. Perhaps most important, they raised the money needed to underwrite the enterprise—$14,500. Much of that was the anonymous gift of Mr. and Mrs. J. Malcolm Forbes, friends of founding faculty member Theodore Dreier and distant relatives of the Steve Forbes who sought the Republican presidential nod in 1996. Even though Rice despised fund-raising, he would spend countless hours at it in his years at Black Mountain. Often candid to a fault, Rice recalled after he left the college that he had to resist the urge to tell potential benefactors, "You've got no business with all that money. Now shell out." That extreme, impolitic candor was one of the characteristics that made Rice a perfect rebel and a considerably less perfect leader.

A crucial decision in shaping Black Mountain was made that first summer when Robert Wunsch, once Thomas Wolfe's roommate at Chapel Hill and later rector of Black Mountain, found a campus for the experimental school. Wunsch suggested that the college try to lease the Blue Ridge Assembly buildings near Asheville.

Used in the summer for YMCA conferences, they stood vacant all winter. A lease was signed, and Black Mountain opened on time, in September 1933.

From the start, the physical setting was an essential part of the Black Mountain experience. The center of life at the new school was Robert E. Lee Hall, a hotel-like three-story building set high on a hill. Although Black Mountain College has been gone for some forty years, you can still stand on the porch of Lee Hall, which continues to host Christian programs each summer, and see what the first collegians saw. The porch's eight grand columns tower above you. But it is the view across the valley of the epic sky and rolling Blue Ridge Mountains that takes your breath away. At night, the sky is packed with stars, as the sky is only where the city is far away. In spring, the dogwoods bloom. The rest of the world seems very distant on the isolated campus. At Black Mountain, radios were rare until World War II turned everyone in the United States into an obsessional listener, and so were clocks. As members of Great Groups so often do, people at Black Mountain could, and often did, focus all their energies on the business of Black Mountain. The relationships and responsibilities that characterized life in the larger society could be put aside here, for better or for worse.

Although Josef Albers and Charles Olson would become charismatic leaders of Black Mountain later in its history, the vision that shaped the college was that of John Andrew Rice. A friend of educational philosopher John Dewey, who made several visits to the school, Rice believed that learning was a process that continued as long as a man or woman breathed. It took place, not just in the classroom, but in the studio, out of doors, in the dining room, wherever people met and shared ideas. According to Duberman, one of the school's favorite adages was that "as much real education took place over the coffee cups as in the classrooms." Like Dewey, Rice had a holistic, some would say anti-intellectual, view of education as a process of personal growth. For Rice, the arts and personal evolution were as important as ideas. As he wrote in *Harper's* in 1937 in a debate with conservative educator Robert Maynard Hutchins, "To know is not enough." (Poet-photographer Jonathan Williams, who was at Black Mountain in the '50s and still lives nearby in Highlands, writes in much the same vein, "Never take know for an answer.")

Like Walt Disney, the plump and bespectacled Rice was not physically imposing. According to his friend Yugoslav writer Louis Adamic, Rice "might be taken for a small-town doctor who has contempt for the rules of diet he prescribes for others." Black Mountain was a community as well as a college, and, in theory at least, everyone, including students, had a say in its affairs. But throughout its early years, Rice was the dominant figure, its paterfamilias, albeit one who often bullied others in the group. In the discussions that were the heart of the Black Mountain experience, Rice often got his way, not by force of logic, but by deploying his charisma like a tank. As Duberman writes, "He overwhelmed, he didn't persuade." But Black Mountain was different from many other Great Groups. It was an intentional community, whose continued existence depended to some degree on consensus, not a company, such as Disney, which could be run by fiat. Rice's failure to persuade would ultimately lead to his loss of power within the group and his expulsion from the academic Eden that he, more than anyone, helped create.

But that was still to come. In the school's first months, led by Rice, Black Mountain adopted a unique structure, with no president, deans, or outside board of trustees, only a rector with limited powers and a board of fellows elected by the group. Decisions were made after long—endless, some would say—debates, in which everyone could speak. Students and faculty, men and women lived in the same building. All meals were taken together, and, probably most significant, everyone's behavior and quality of mind were under more or less constant scrutiny by everyone else.

The curriculum was equally unusual. Students chose their own courses of study, in consultation with the faculty. Students continued in the lower or Junior Division until they felt they had experienced various disciplines widely enough to move on to the Senior Division, where specialization began, tailored to the individual student. Students had to pass oral and written exams before moving up. When a student felt ready to graduate, he or she submitted a statement of accomplishment to the faculty. If it was accepted, the student was tested, in front of anyone from the college who wished to participate, by a group of outside examiners, which included, over the years, such notables as Jacques Barzun, Paul Goodman, Franz Kline, and Marcel Breuer. But at Black Mountain, process was far more important than anything as conventional as a diploma. Only fifty or so students ever bothered to graduate.

So many Great Groups exist as enclaves of excellence in surroundings with which they have little in common. Like the scientists of the Manhattan Project in remote Los Alamos, the educational rebels of Black Mountain were strangers in a strange land. Nearby Asheville was a small city of considerable sophistication, but Black Mountain was back in the hills, in woods full of black bears, moonshiners, and members of snake-handling cults. The faculty and students were out of sync with their mountain neighbors on virtually every-thing, from their views on churchgoing and the rights of African Americans to their attitudes toward sex and politics. Rumors about free love, free thinking, Com-munism, and who knows what else began to circulate almost as soon as the school opened. (In fact, there was not a great deal of overt sexual activity in the early years, and old-timers at a 1995 Black Mountain re-union were visibly horrified at writer Fielding Daw-son's recollections of bisexual shenanigans in the late years.) On one occasion, a local milkman glanced through a window in Lee Hall and saw a class of stu-dents drawing a nude model. If that weren't sufficiently scandalous, students shocked the townsfolk by doing their shopping wearing sandals. The locals took to call-ing the college people "the mentals."

At Black Mountain, as in other Great Groups, one of the leader's most important tasks was recruiting. Rice made at least one superb choice in artist Josef Albers. In 1933, Albers was in Berlin, the worst of all places for a modern artist (the Nazis preferred the term *degenerate artist*), especially one married to a Jew, weaver Anni Albers. Great Groups have a tendency to give rise to others. Some would argue, not quite accurately, that the Bauhaus begat Black Mountain. It is true that Albers taught and worked at the legendary German in-stitution, where the integration of form and function and other principles of modern design were being hammered out, until it closed in 1933 rather than submit to the strictures of the Third Reich. But from the start, the guiding spirit of Black Mountain was the aggressive, ornery, utterly American vision of Rice. Nonetheless, Black Mountain artist and teacher Ilya Bolotowsky would later joke that the college was "the outhouse of the Bauhaus."

According to Duberman, Rice said in the college's first months, "Don't ask me how or why I know it, but I know it: if I can't get the right man for art, then the thing won't work." Rice wanted art to be the soul of the curriculum at Black Mountain, but not art in the narrow sense of the techniques of drawing, painting, or sculpture or even of classical aesthetics. He wanted someone who could teach art as both a discipline and a way of experiencing the world. Rice sought the advice of Philip Johnson, then curator of architecture at the Museum of Modern Art in Manhattan. Johnson, who had been impressed with Albers's teaching during a visit to the Bauhaus and who knew the artist was eager to leave Germany, suggested him for the post. Rice knew at once that Albers was his man because Johnson praised Albers's teaching so passionately. "But he does have one defect," Johnson warned. "Albers doesn't speak a word of English." Unfazed, Rice authorized Johnson to hire both the Alberses at once.

Albers, who never fully mastered English, had doubts, even if Rice did not. Later, Albers recalled that he was both fearful about going to the United States and glad to leave Germany: "no pumpernickel, such red and green drinks in America. All I knew was Buster Keaton and Henry Ford. I spoke no English."

At Black Mountain, both teachers and students flocked to the most exciting classes. Certain courses loom very large in the memories of Black Mountain people, including Alfred Kazin's course on *Moby Dick* during the mid-1940s. But it was Albers's courses on materials, color, and the elements of form that became the very heart of the curriculum, just as Rice had hoped. Johnson had warned Rice that Albers's teaching method was difficult to describe. Again and again, former students and faculty have tried and failed to put into words exactly what Albers did in class and the impact it had on his students. When asked on his arrival in the United States what he hoped to achieve, Albers responded, "To open eyes." In that, he succeeded to an extraordinary degree.

Albers said his goal was "to direct eyes in observation—know what you are seeing and know why you are seeing this, and how to lubricate your fingers and hands and arms to visualize it on paper or the blackboard or whatever you have in your hand." In class, Albers used a hands-on method to teach key ideas. He believed, Duberman writes, that the nature of an object is made up of three aspects: its inner qualities, its external appearance, and how it relates to other objects. Duberman describes how Albers would have the students explore the nature of paper, for instance. Students would fold it, pin it, and create three-dimensional objects with it to discover its strength and other properties. Each student would come up with a personal solution to the problem of a sheet of paper. Albers would critique them, sometimes harshly, as would other members of the class. Finally, Albers would have the students unfold the paper, smooth it out, and return it to its original state.

Dogmatic and rather puritanical in his views, Albers did not preach self-expression. The seer's job was to observe and then to "train the pencil to do what your eyes see." Color was a passion of Albers ("Color, I think, was his only love," Rice wrote later), and Albers taught it by showing how hues completely transformed each other when juxtaposed. Perhaps most famous of all were the exercises he called *matière* studies. Students had to find the materials, then explore such questions as how one material could be made to look like another and how surfaces differed, corresponded, and could be combined in interesting ways. The late James Hall, a writer and educator who was a student at Black Mountain in 1940–41, recalled one of his own *matière* studies: "I distinctly remember assembling on a tray some orange-topped mushrooms, a rusty bed-spring, and some blackened pieces of toast. We brought our 'compositions' to class, slowly paraded them around the room, sneering at everybody else's. The generally elicited comment that my composition was too somber led me to offer to scrape the toast a little."

Many of those involved with Black Mountain say that their courses with Albers changed their lives. Artist Margaret Kennard Johnson studied with Albers during the remarkable summer of 1944. "For the first time," she recalled, "I learned that painting, sculpture, architecture, drawing, designing were not separately wrapped packages, but all were forms of the same visual language." Although she worked at Black Mountain for only six weeks, Johnson believed her universally applicable training there is what allowed her subsequently to immerse herself quickly in the unfamiliar world of Japanese art.

Although many students adored Albers, others found him inflexible and stifling. Often the most talented student artists were the ones who found his autocratic classroom style most offensive. Robert De Niro, the late painter father of actor Robert De Niro, became so furious after a chilly encounter with Albers that he tossed all his possessions, including his art supplies, out the window of his third-floor room in Lee Hall and quit the college on the spot.

As Mary Emma Harris makes clear in *The Arts at Black Mountain College,* Rice and Albers were both vital to their Great Group. According to Adamic, Rice was Black Mountain's "center, its core," and Albers "the strongest diffused influence on the place." In Dreier's view, "Rice is the man who makes the college a continuing possibility . . . but Albers is the one who makes it turn out to be what it is more than Rice or anybody else realizes."

In the early years at least, Rice and Albers functioned to some degree as dual leaders, much as Oppenheimer and Groves did for the Manhattan Project. Rice and Albers were both men of stature, respected by the group and respectful of each other. Whereas the original vision was clearly Rice's, it was congruous with Albers's own strong convictions about art and education and it was a vision that Albers quickly adopted and promulgated. In their different spheres, Rice and Albers both performed another important role typical of leaders of Great Groups. They served as conduits of information between the group and the larger world. Black Mountain might be a poor, isolated school in Appalachia, but, through Rice, it attracted the attention and input of Dewey, writer Thorton Wilder, and others who, in turn, brought Black Mountain to the attention of the world at large (Eleanor Roosevelt was among its distinguished visitors). Albers was wired into the art world both abroad and in the United States and indeed had an enviable network of contacts in every corner of the avant-garde. Later, Charles Olson, too, would draw talent to the school and keep Black Mountain in the consciousness of the country's artistic movers and shakers, to an extraordinary degree given its dwindling size and worsening poverty.

From its first day, the lifeblood of Black Mountain was talk. A number of memoirs of the college refer to it as an eccentric kind of monastery. That image may be accurate in capturing the sense of common purpose and community that pervaded the school, but it is misleading in one respect. Nobody at Black Mountain ever took a vow of silence. Even the people who spoke poor English spoke it frequently and vociferously. Black Mountain was unlike most other Great Groups in that its mission was not the development of a new thing— an atomic bomb, *Snow White and the Seven Dwarfs,* or a user-friendly computer. The project in which everyone at Black Mountain was ostensibly engaged was building the community and personal growth. In the best of all possible worlds, community and individual growth are complementary goals, not incompatible ones. But Black Mountain was often not the best of all possible worlds. It was a changing group of opinionated, articulate people possessed of varying degrees of talent and of variable character. Since the college saw talk as the proper medium for achieving its goals, long group meetings were a fixture of campus life. At their best, these meetings were forums for the exchange of insights and ideas on such lofty issues as the nature of art and how freedom and responsibility can be reconciled. At their worst, they were embarrassing performances by squabbling prima donnas, perfect illustrations of Emerson's observation that "almost all people descend to meet."

At Black Mountain, all the passion and tenacity that other Great Groups brought to building a stealth bomber or inventing a computer went into meetings of the group. Duberman's account of how Rice came to leave the college in 1940 includes transcripts of some of the most contentious and significant of these meetings. One of the most original and controversial aspects of life at Black Mountain was the collective discussion of personnel issues (although decisions were not always made collectively). In 1936–37, the school was roiled by the emergence of rival factions: one centered on Rice, the other centered on psychologist Irving Knickerbocker, who had just received his Ph.D. from Harvard when he was hired in 1935. Rice, who proudly acknowledged that he was often prickly, had long had a troubled relationship with some in the community, including students, who thought he talked a better game about shared decision making than he actually played. Rice's worst detractors thought he had become the Black Mountain equivalent of his autocratic nemesis, Rollins's President, Hamilton Holt. But Knickerbocker, whose specialty was troubled children, challenged Rice in a more subtle way. Knickerbocker told faculty and students that Rice was a destructive presence in the community, one whose candor was as likely to destroy a student as to bring about the personal growth that was the stated reason for Rice's often scathing critiques.

Rice accused Knickerbocker of coddling students and of conducting a whispering campaign against him (the latter charge was true). The immediate result of the campus power struggle was that Knickerbocker was asked to leave at the end of the 1936–37 year. Knickerbocker subsequently joined the faculty at Antioch College, where, with Douglas McGregor, he developed its distinguished program in group dynamics. But the group dynamic during the wrangle between Rice and Knickerbocker epitomized Black Mountain at its most dystopian. It is also a vivid reminder that most Great Groups are project driven and that the intensity that characterizes them can tear them apart in the absence of something solid and external to the members to unify and ground them.

Knickerbocker was followed out of Black Mountain by about a third of the faculty and students, the first in a series of mass departures that would characterize the school as surely as its roster of outstanding members (critic Eric Bentley led a notable walkout in 1944). Even with Knickerbocker gone, Rice's reputation never recovered. The proximate cause of his downfall was most pedestrian: "I fell for a slut," Rice said later of his affair with a student. The relationship greatly distressed Rice's wife, Nell, a popular member of the community (and the college's librarian in later years) and eventually led Rice to resign—just as the board of fellows was about to declare officially that he was no longer welcome. Observers say Rice's vision continued to shape Black Mountain as long as it existed. But one immediate result of his departure was to magnify the role that Albers played at the college, until he, too, left, in 1949, to become chairman of a new art department at Yale.

Rice is a good example of a critically flawed leader of a Great Group. Rice had a powerful and original vision, and the charisma to instill that vision in others. But, ultimately, he was perceived as lacking the character that members of Great Groups demand of their leaders. Rice was narcissistic. He could be cruel, arbitrary, even petty. Like most Great Groups, Black Mountain was a place where leadership had little or nothing to do with title or official role. Even when Rice was not rector of the college, he had been its head, its heart. Orit Gadiesh, chairman of the Boston management consulting firm of Bain & Company, has said that the most important thing a leader can have is a sense of "true north." That, she explains, "is a set of principles that directs him or her to what's virtuous or right." Leadership always comes down to a question of character. If Rice had continued to be perceived by the others at Black Mountain as possessing true north, it's unlikely that any covert campaign or any act of adultery would have toppled him.

Although its mission was never as clear as that of groups involved in creating an actual thing, Black Mountain was a place that throbbed with the excitement of creating something new. All Great Groups are boundary busters, and Black Mountain, with its unusual curriculum and changing cast of fascinating characters, was no exception. Under the terms of the school's lease with the Blue Ridge Assembly, the college had to pack all its furniture and other belongings away in the attic each spring so that church conferences could take place throughout the summer. The result, Martin Duberman observes, was that every fall the college had a sense of starting from scratch, almost literally, as people scrambled to find furniture for their rooms. As in other Great Groups, the negatives of high pressure and uncertainty were offset at Black Mountain by the joy of discovery. "Every morning the world seems to start all over again," composer Frederic "Fritz" Cohen wrote when he was teaching at Black Mountain in the early 1940s. "Every bit of past experience, of tradition, of accepted rule and law is questioned constantly." Writer Fielding Dawson, a student there during the literary renaissance of the '50s, remembers how rich and heady was the sense of accomplishing something new and wonderful. "We knew we were on the cutting edge," he told an interviewer. "We knew then that we were making history."

Although faculty of Black Mountain were often brought in by Rice, Albers, Olson, or one of the other campus leaders, students were largely self-selected. Only a certain kind of person fit in at Black Mountain—a person who was talented, thick-skinned, and unintimidated by a milking machine was the ideal candidate. Dawson recalls the process: "People would visit Black Mountain and return home and say, 'You'—meaning 'You oddball'—would really like it there."

The educational experience was undiluted at Black Mountain. People rarely left the campus on weekends, especially in the early years, and you could never get away from the rest of the community for long. That kind of collective intensity drove some people away—critic Edward Dahlberg lasted only two weeks. The physical conditions were often harsh as well. The college was never luxurious, despite the beauty of the setting, and at times it offered all the comforts of boot camp. Mildred Adams Harding was a faculty wife there in the early 1950s, and she recalls suffering through a bitterly cold winter in an unheated cabin. Food was in such short supply that she was genuinely concerned that her two babies might get scurvy. Harding and her husband left Black Mountain after a year to join the faculty at the American University in Cairo, Egypt. The administrator who hired them remarked, "If those two can survive Black Mountain College and laugh about it, they're tough enough for Egypt."

The greatest irritant at Black Mountain seems to have been the same as its greatest strength—the idiosyncratic group of people, many of them greatly talented, who came together there. As Duberman observes, "There was a great deal more 'self-expression' at Black Mountain than selves to express; or, as one disillusioned Olsonite put it, 'There's not enough character here and there's too much personality.' " Jonathan Williams wrote recently that his army training as a psychiatric worker served him well at Black Mountain, especially in dealing with his fellow poets. As Williams makes clear, Black Mountain wasn't always Eden, the name of the college lake notwithstanding. "There were a lot of bad days, too . . . Creeley, Olson, Dorn, Wieners, Dawson—zounds! Please pass the Prozac!"

But there is nothing like a shared ordeal to build cohesion, as armies and fraternities have long known. Those who stayed at Black Mountain and went through the fire together developed a heightened sense of kinship. Many who were there say the experience set them apart from the rest of the world and continues to do so. Dawson's belief is that if you weren't at Black Mountain, you simply cannot understand what it was all about.

Great Groups often have a decidedly adolescent side. At Black Mountain, the art students particularly seemed to have great fun devising ways to puncture the pretensions of their stern mentor, Josef Albers. Almost inevitably, one of the *matière* studies put before the master was composed of campus cow dung. In another famous incident in the late '40s, a number of the school's most talented young artists, including Kenneth Noland and Joseph Fiore, began meeting after classes in Stan Hebel's room and applying whatever was left on their palettes to a large canvas hung on his wall. After a year, according to participant Jerrold Levy, their collaborative canvas looked "like something between a Motherwell and a de Kooning." As Duberman recounts, the young men signed the painting "Anonymous Blotch" and hung it in the dining room. The incident occurred during one of the periodic outbreaks of factionalism on campus, and Albers, who had been feuding with their teacher, Bolotowsky, was gratifyingly furious.

Black Mountain had started a farm during its first year, and, despite Rice's lack of enthusiasm for obligatory physical labor, the work program became a signature of the school. Black Mountain students and faculty worked side by side doing all the things that had to be done on campus, from building and maintaining roads to growing crops and tending cattle. Students made the back-strap looms for Anni Albers's classes, built their own furniture, worked in the print shop, and anticipated Martha Stewart in crafting imaginative tableware for college feasts (the women also took to fashioning willowy dresses from flour sacks to wear to the popular Saturday night dances). During World War II they briefly mined mica on campus, standing in icy water up to their calves. They planted corn and hacked it down with machetes for silage. And when beloved music teacher Heinrich Jalowetz died suddenly in 1946, they dug his grave and hauled a stone to mark it. But, most remarkably, beginning in 1940, they built their own school.

Building the new campus seems to have been the shining moment in Black Mountain's history. During the several years that the community worked brutally hard to put up the Studies Building and remodel other campus buildings, the group was united as never before. Great Groups need tangible projects. They can coalesce only around something to which every member contributes but that exists outside the minds of the members, something that can only be achieved collectively.

Black Mountain had been seeking a new campus almost from its founding. Always in danger of losing its lease with the Blue Ridge Assembly, the college had bought a former summer resort in 1937 with an eye to turning it into a permanent campus. Located a few miles from the original site, in an area more bucolic and less dramatic than the Assembly grounds, the new site had a man-made lake—Lake Eden—two unheated lodges, and other buildings spread out on 667 acres.

Because of their friendship with Albers, former Bauhaus architects Walter Gropius and Marcel Breuer designed a new, multipurpose building complex for the college. But because of lack of funds, the school opted for a simpler design—a single, multiuse building, which had classrooms, studios, and storerooms on the lower floors and student and faculty housing upstairs. Dubbed the Studies Building, the structure was begun in 1940 and was sufficiently finished by the spring of 1941 to be occupied. Each day during construction, the faculty and students sang folk songs as they went off to cut down oak trees, work stone, and pour concrete. Although someone posted a sign on a campus bulletin board that read, "Wanted: Zombies for the work program," most of the amateur builders remember that time as one of the most rewarding and tranquil in the school's history.

Today, the second site of Black Mountain is used as a boys' camp, but the Studies Building remains. If you look closely, you can see the frescoes, now terribly faded, that artist Jean Charlot painted on the foundation supports under the building. In the summer of 1944, Ruth Lyford Sussler, later a painter, was one of the students who helped mix and shovel the wet cement on which Charlot painted. That unforgettable summer, Sussler heard Agnes de Mille lecture authoritatively on dance. Sussler saw her first "Coloreds Only" water fountain in town and her first chain gang. And she fondly remembers taking "musical" baths in an old-fashioned, claw-footed tub in the girls' dorm, with the sounds of a string bass practicing chamber music in the room below rising up through the floorboards. With its typical Black Mountain mix of physical work, immersion in the arts, and a sense of being transported to another planet (the rural South), that summer, Sussler recalls, "was crucial to my whole subsequent existence."

Black Mountain wasn't simply a place where creative collaboration took place. It was *about* creative collaboration. One of the shaping principles of the college was that art and education were group processes, not solitary ones. A fine example of that philosophy was the campus production during the summer of 1948 of Erik

Satie's play *The Ruse of Medusa*. That summer was an especially exciting one. John Cage gave twenty-five concerts of Satie's music, most of them in the intimate venue of his cottage. It was Cage who asked Mary Caroline ("M. C.") Richards, the poet and ceramicist and one of the school's most popular teachers, to do an English translation of the slight Satie work, which had been performed only once before, in Paris.

Fielding Dawson once observed that at Black Mountain "so many were involved in the production of plays that very few were able to see them." *The Ruse of Medusa* was a typical Black Mountain production, the startlingly original work of a group of talented people, many working outside their specialties. Buckminster Fuller was cast in the lead as Baron Medusa, whom painter Elaine de Kooning, who played his daughter, described as "a kind of W. C. Fields aristocrat who talked constantly in non sequiturs." Poet Isaac Rosenfeld played the surly butler. Willem de Kooning designed the set, using paint to make a desk and two ordinary columns look like marvels of pink and gray marble. Cage played the Satie score, and Merce Cunningham created and performed entr'acte dances in the guise of a mechanical monkey.

Great Groups tend to be nonhierarchical. Members make contributions based on talent, not on role. This ad hoc theatrical company was no exception. The director was a gifted student, Arthur Penn, who had begun offering theater courses on campus. The key to the success of the play was the remarkable transformation Penn was able to facilitate in Fuller. A famously ebullient man, Fuller was initially stiff and uncomfortable as an actor. Fuller admitted to Penn that he was "afraid of making a damn fool of myself" on stage. Penn decided Fuller needed to see that making a damn fool of himself wouldn't be so awful, and so, during rehearsal, the young man joined the creator of the geodesic dome in doing just that—skipping, rolling around together, and generally acting foolish. As Duberman writes, "From that point on, Bucky blossomed." Fuller said later that he owed much of his subsequent success as a lecturer to Penn, who taught him how to be natural on stage. Years later, when Fuller was nervous about getting an honorary doctorate from Harvard, which had expelled him as an undergraduate, he met with Penn, who prepared Fuller for the important occasion by reviewing the lessons of the Satie play.

Although the collaboration resulted in a single performance, it appears to have transformed several lives. Penn said years later that he had learned an enormous amount from doing the play. Working closely with other creative people at Black Mountain, artists often experienced accelerated creative growth. Working with Cage and Cunningham, Penn said, he considered exciting new theatrical possibilities for the first time, such as moving the action into the auditorium. More important, Cage and Cunningham gave Penn creative courage he might otherwise not have had, especially given his youth. As Penn told Duberman, "They breathed liberty into that whole experience . . . 'Risk that!' 'Change this!' 'Don't feel that audience effect is the dictator of what should be produced.'" Penn said a decade passed before he realized how profoundly the experience had influenced him.

Although only a few such collaborations became famous, notably the 1952 "happening" that involved

Cage, Cunningham, Robert Rauschenberg, Charles Olson, and M. C. Richards, among others, group creativity was an ongoing feature of Black Mountain life. Also typical of Black Mountain was the assumption that students had things to teach their teachers. Dawson would later write of his mentor, "Olson learned so much from each one of us. He really needed us. We changed him. He learned how to teach from us." Great Groups are typically places where gifted neophytes interact on an equal footing with older, more famous colleagues, as young Richard Feynman did at Los Alamos with the great Danish physicist Niels Bohr.

The late Charles Olson led Black Mountain through its final flourishing and oversaw its demise. Described by Jonathan Williams as "a vast, energetic spectacle," Olson was six-foot-seven and weighed 250 pounds or more. The huge poet was, as Duberman writes, "unquestionably the heartbeat of Black Mountain during its last five years." Leaders of Great Groups function as catalysts, and they also often mediate between the outside world and the inside world of the group. What Albers did for Black Mountain as a community emphasizing the visual arts, Olson did for it as a literary community.

Writers had not always found Black Mountain particularly fertile ground. Kazin, who taught there briefly in the mid-1940s, complained, "If you were a serious writer, Black Mountain could be in many ways a very half-assed place." But Olson changed that, and, during his tenure, the college became a magnet for writers, particularly poets, and even gave its name to a school of poets that includes Olson, Creeley, Robert Duncan, Jonathan Williams, and others.

Although Olson would have found the comparison decidedly unhip, he had certain leadership qualities in common with Walt Disney. Olson had some gift as a writer, but his real genius was for sniffing out talent in others and instilling in them his vision of the collective enterprise. As he told Duberman, Olson was able to revitalize Black Mountain creatively, if not fiscally, by returning to what he called "the core of the old apple," Rice's original vision of a curriculum with the arts as its center. Olson also rallied his followers by denouncing the New Criticism and other forces of yesterday and calling for a new, distinctively American literature that emphasized authenticity of voice.

Olson didn't care that the Black Mountain campus was in increasing disrepair. As in so many other Great Groups, from the jerry-built labs of the Manhattan Project to the makeshift headquarters of the Macintosh group, the spirit flourished in buildings that were gimcrack and shabby. Olson boldly declared that "such poverty-stricken ambiance is the one fit for living, for working." Writer Michael Rumaker, one of the minority of students who actually graduated from Black Mountain, in 1955, remembers how his first visit to the deteriorating campus was made golden by the intensity and clarity of Olson's vision. "Charles's talk was an artful and seductive sales pitch. . . . But the substance of his talk went well beyond that. The possibilities and vision he expressed about Black Mountain took on the excitement of an adventurous crusade, a sacred vision, that he intimated . . . [I] would be privileged to participate in."

Conditions on campus became increasingly desperate. At one point, Duberman reports, in hopes of getting approval to enroll Korean War vets, the college tried to trick inspectors from the Veterans Administration into thinking there were more than a handful of students left on campus. The same pitifully small group of students was shifted from classroom to classroom, with costume changes in between. But Olson never stopped dreaming on a grand scale or articulating the dream. Even as the college was breaking up in 1956, Olson was negotiating with painter Richard Diebenkorn to join the faculty.

The Olson years were among the most passionate and memorable in the school's history. But faculty and many of the most gifted students began to drift elsewhere. San Francisco, with its Beat scene, was an alternative mecca. In 1955, the school was threatened with foreclosure by former patron J. Malcolm Forbes, who held the first mortgage. Black Mountain was able to come up with the money to prevent foreclosure, but a new threat emerged when some former faculty and staff, including Nell Rice, threatened to sue for back pay. They, too, were put off. Finally, the college faced the remote but real possibility that the state of North Carolina would close it down because of alleged immorality. A student was charged with living on campus with a woman who was not his wife. True, he said, but the rector, Olson, also lives here with a woman other than his wife. (Olson had left Connie Olson, his common-law wife and mother of their daughter, Katie, for Black Mountain student Betty Kaiser. Olson and Kaiser were living on campus with their infant son, Charles Peter.) Moreover, the student said, some of the men on campus have sex with other men. Clearly, the college had changed from the school that had exiled Rice because of his adultery and had forced former rector Robert Wunsch to sneak off in the middle of the night in 1945 after he was charged with a morals violation involving a local marine.

None of these factors actually forced the school to close, Olson later told Duberman. In 1956, Black Mountain just sort of fizzled out. Olson and another of the school's administrators decided the time had come to disband. Olson remained for six months to dispose of Rice's papers and to finish up other college business. Olson and several other Black Mountain poets, including Creeley, later moved to the State University of New York at Buffalo, where in the mid-1960s that institution briefly flirted with the idea of creating residential colleges, some in the Black Mountain mold. Olson, who died in 1970, suggested to Duberman that the college continued on through the people who had been there and took some of Black Mountain with them when they dispersed. Olson wrote to Duberman, "There is no end to the story, her flag flies."

There was considerable truth to Olson's remark. Black Mountain had a profound and continuing effect on many of the people it touched, including Duberman, who was inspired to write a highly creative history of the school that combines traditional research with a personal analysis of the process. When he finished writing the book, Duberman found himself near tears, for "all those extraordinary people, their foolishness, their valor, their *trying.*" Surely, some of the spirit of the place survived in the communes and other countercultural institutions that flowered a decade after Black Mountain closed its doors.

In 1995, about 150 former faculty and staff of Black Mountain attended a reunion on the Lake Eden campus.

It was organized by Mary Holden, a young photographer who first heard about Black Mountain College from artist friends in Paris. Now a resident of the town of Black Mountain, she is the founder of the Black Mountain College Museum & Arts Center, currently housed in temporary space in Asheville. In the course of the reunion, the former collegians did what they had always done. They argued at great length over whether a Black Mountain museum was a violation of the very spirit of the place, as contrary to the original, anti-institutional nature of Black Mountain as a museum of Dada.

THE MANHATTAN PROJECT

In the study of Great Groups a few names turn up again and again. Remember Vannevar Bush? It was his speculative article, "As We May Think," published in the *Atlantic Monthly* in 1945, that started Douglas Engelbart thinking about a personal machine for storing and accessing information, which led, almost thirty years later, to the user-friendly computer. And, in the spring of 1940, as Americans confronted the increasing likelihood of going to war against Hitler, Bush was pondering another question that would lead to an extraordinary collaboration: how to make sure that a United States on the verge of war benefited fully from the scientific brainpower available to it.

An engineer, inventor, and educator, as well as president of the Carnegie Institution, Bush knew that without some effective link between government and science, ideas and technology that could affect the outcome of the war might be lost. He knew because he had experienced firsthand what lack of such coordination could mean. During World War I, Bush worked for a research firm that invented a magnetic submarine detector. A hundred of the devices had actually been produced. But because of what Richard Rhodes describes in his monumental history, *The Making of the Atomic Bomb,* as "bureaucratic confusion," the detectors were never used in action. Determined to see his country exploit recent discoveries in nuclear fission in particular, Bush lobbied for the creation of a National Defense Research Council that would work with the military but would be independent of it. With the help of Roosevelt confidant Harry Hopkins, Bush got the president's approval for the NDRC in less than ten minutes.

The story of the building of the atomic bomb has been told in almost as much detail as that of the Battle of Gettysburg. But it was Bush, rather than far more famous figures such as Einstein and Oppenheimer, who had the vision that allowed the United States, working closely with the British, to create, in only three years, the weapon that would end the war (as well as threaten humanity with annihilation). Bush wanted to make sure that the full cycle of collaboration was completed—that great science and technology moved beyond the theoretical to make a difference in the world. In retrospect, the decision to build the bomb was fraught with agonizing ambiguities. But in 1940, a war against Hitler seemed as close to a just war as any in history. Bush's council ensured that nonmilitary voices were heard in Washington and maximized the chances of a successful scientific-military collaboration.

Whatever reservations the individual scientists had about making weapons, few had any doubts about the genius of such German nuclear physicists as Werner Heisenberg, nor about the ruthlessness of Hitler's regime. Ironically, Hitler himself had aided what would become the Allied effort, not only by serving as a diabolical enemy to rally against, but by driving out so many of Germany's best scientists because they were

Jewish. Until the Manhattan Project was well under way, Bush and most of the top scientists involved believed that the Germans might be able to build the bomb first. Preventing that was a sufficiently holy cause to make all but a handful of scientists sign up for a project that would offer daunting intellectual challenges but would take them far, both physically and morally, from their peacetime labs and offices.

Day-to-day responsibility for the building of the atomic bomb would lie in the hands of as odd a couple as U.S. history has known. In August 1942, Bush approached Brehon Somervell, the general in charge of Army Services of Supply, asking him to recommend someone in the military who could expedite the enormous effort that would be required for the bomb project. Somervell knew just the man. Leslie R. Groves was a forty-six-year-old colonel in the Army Corps of Engineers. That he could get things done was a given: as deputy chief of construction for the army, he had just completed his biggest project to date, the building of the Pentagon. A big man, just under six feet tall and upward of 250 pounds, he was blunt, tireless, and unusually competent. Typical of his foresight, he suggested that he not be appointed until after his promotion to brigadier general. "I thought that there might be some problems in dealing with the many academic scientists involved in the project," he recalled in 1962, "and I felt that my position would be stronger if they thought of me from the first as a general instead of as a promoted colonel."

It was Groves who wanted Oppenheimer for the Manhattan Project (so-called because the first efforts had taken place within the Corps of Engineers' Manhattan

Engineer District). Whereas Groves was repeatedly described as a bear of a man, thirty-eight-year-old Oppenheimer was nervous and painfully thin. A friend from Berkeley noted Oppenheimer's intense blue eyes and said he looked "like a young Einstein, and at the same time like an overgrown choir boy."

Oppenheimer was everything the solidly middle-American Groves was not—a theoretician, a man of culture (he had learned Sanskrit in order to read his beloved Bhagavad Gita), a nonobservant Jew, and a leftist. On the faculties of both Berkeley and Cal Tech, Oppenheimer was highly regarded by his peers, although he had no Nobel Prize, as Enrico Fermi and others had. He also lacked experience leading a large group, and he was sometimes abrasive and patronizing.

It is a measure of Groves's pragmatic intelligence that he wanted Oppenheimer despite his limitations, including the fact that his wife, Kitty, and brother had been members of the Communist Party. As Rhodes reports, Groves shared Oppenheimer's view that the project needed a central lab where the scattered group, currently working at the University of Chicago and other sites, would be able to work side by side on the complex problems that had to be solved before the theory of nuclear fission could be translated into a viable weapon. Groves wanted Oppenheimer because, the newly minted general said, "He's a genius. . . . Oppenheimer knows about everything. He can talk to you about anything you bring up. Well, not exactly. I guess there are a few things he doesn't know about. He doesn't know anything about sports." Undaunted by Oppie's inability to rattle off ball scores, Groves recommended Oppenheimer to the Military Policy Committee. Predictably, they nixed Oppenheimer. But in this, too, Groves showed his acumen by asking them to come up with the names of better choices. When they failed, Oppenheimer was in.

Groves and Oppenheimer had complementary virtues that allowed them to work independently and efficiently toward the same goal. Oppenheimer reported to Groves, whose office remained in Washington, D.C. Oppenheimer would recruit the scientists for the project and would be in charge of coordinating the group, which Groves believed, correctly, would include a number of "prima donnas," at the project's new secret lab. Every generous inch a military man, Groves made important concessions to Oppenheimer in the interest of getting the job done. Groves had wanted all the scientists to have army commissions in order to maximize government control, including security. He had also wanted compartmentalization, so that scientists working on one part of the project could not share information with any other team. But Oppenheimer soon discovered that physicist I. I. Rabi and others balked at militarization. If the scientists could not retain their scientific autonomy, Oppenheimer told Washington, some would refuse to join the project. Oppenheimer also knew that science cannot proceed without the free exchange of information. Without openness, the crucial problems might never be discovered, solutions might never be found. Openness would also bolster morale. Both Groves and Oppenheimer were men with considerable egos. But, in a compelling common cause, they were able to transcend their egos and negotiate a compromise. They agreed that the scientists would retain their traditional freedom to share information with anyone else in the group, but that the group itself would be isolated from the rest of the world, at a remote site behind a guarded, barbed-wire fence.

That site was, of course, Los Alamos, New Mexico. Great Groups tend to be islands of excellence that exist apart from their surroundings. But Los Alamos was isolated in the extreme. Located thirty-five miles outside Santa Fe, Los Alamos was chosen because it was far from the coasts and national borders thought vulnerable to enemy invasion, far from population centers, and yet close to good transportation. It was also in the New Mexico wilderness that Oppenheimer had loved since he first went there as a sickly teenager. As an adult, he had a vacation home nearby. When Groves and Oppenheimer first visited the site together in November 1942, there was nothing there but a boys' school, whose hardy students and staff wore shorts as they played outside in a light snowfall. As physicist John Manley noted afterward, "Many people have the idea that Los Alamos was in the desert area of New Mexico. In fact, the school was on a mesa amidst magnificent scenery . . . it is a very attractive place with lots of good places to hike and stroll and scenery to enjoy." After buying the property, the army kept the lodge and other existing school buildings and began a crash program to build labs, housing, and other facilities for a community that quickly grew from a few hundred to a wartime high of more than 2,100 scientists, support personnel, and their families. Eventually, the population soared past 10,000.

A primitive ski run was one of the few amenities of the original Los Alamos Ranch School. Like horseback riding, skiing was quickly taken up by the residents of the new community. Inevitably, the scientists used some of the same ingenuity they brought to building the bomb to improving their high-desert outpost. Chemist George Kistiakowsky, who did some of the most important explosives work for the implosion bomb, devised a creative way to cut down trees to improve the ski run. He used surplus plastic explosive. "If one builds a half necklace around the tree," he explained, "then the explosion cuts it as if it were a chain saw—and it's faster. A little noisier, though."

In a collection of reminiscences of wartime Los Alamos, editors Lawrence Badash, Joseph O. Hirschfelder, and Herbert P. Broida observe that "more scientific talent was accumulated there than at any time since Isaac Newton dined alone." Oppenheimer traveled around the country recruiting, but he usually had an easy sell, despite the remoteness of Los Alamos and the burdens that secrecy would put on the recruits and their families. As Oppenheimer wrote later, yes, many were put off by the military nature of the project and "the notion of disappearing into the New Mexico desert for an indeterminate period. . . . But there was another side to it. Almost everyone realized that this was a great undertaking. Almost everyone knew that if it were completed successfully and rapidly enough, it might determine the outcome of the war. Almost everyone knew that it was an unparalleled opportunity to bring to bear the basic knowledge and art of science for the benefit of his country. Almost everyone knew that this job, if it were achieved, would be part of history. This sense of excitement, of devotion, and of patriotism in the end prevailed. Most of those with whom I talked came to Los Alamos." If talented people can be recruited to make a movie about a put-upon princess and seven dwarfs, is it any wonder, given the soaring stakes at Los Alamos, that people as distinguished as Fermi and Hans Bethe eagerly signed up?

The physicists and chemists who pioneered the field of nuclear physics were a relatively small group who followed each other's work in scholarly journals and piggybacked on it in their own labs. The great Danish physicist Niels Bohr, whose groundbreaking work on quantum theory won him the Nobel Prize in 1922, had instituted international conferences in the field in the 1920s that attracted all the major players, including Heisenberg. Oppenheimer was part of this international circle, and so he began recruiting with a first-rate wish list in hand.

Although the bomb project was supposed to be top secret, some scientists didn't hesitate to reveal more than they should have to bring aboard others whom they respected and trusted. Robert R. Wilson, who had been a student of Oppenheimer's and was teaching at Princeton, was responsible for commandeering Harvard's cyclotron for Los Alamos. Wilson also recruited young Richard Feynman, then a Princeton graduate student. Feynman, who went on to win the Nobel Prize for his work in quantum electrodynamics, recalled the moment years later. Wilson came into Feynman's room and told him that he, Wilson, had been recruited for a secret project to find a way to separate the isotopes of uranium. There was to be a meeting that day at three o'clock. Feynman said he was not interested, but assured Wilson he needn't worry about his telling anyone. Then Feynman recalled, "I went back to work on my thesis— for about three minutes. Then I began to pace the floor and think about this thing. The Germans had Hitler and the possibility of developing an atomic bomb was obvious, and the possibility that they would develop it before we did was very much of a fright. So I decided to go to the meeting at 3 o'clock. By 4 o'clock I already had a desk in a room and was trying to calculate whether this particular method was limited by the total amount of current that you get in an ion beam, and so on. . . . I had a desk, and I had paper, and I was working as hard as I could and as fast as I could, so the fellows who were building the apparatus could do the experiment right there." Although work on the bomb continued at the University of Chicago, where Fermi first produced and controlled nuclear energy in 1942, and several other sites, the cream of Western science increasingly gathered in New Mexico. Feynman was hardly exaggerating when he said, "All science stopped during the war except the little bit that was done at Los Alamos. And that was not much science; it was mostly engineering." The average age of the scientists was twenty-five.

Ruth Marshak, who taught third grade there, recalled that "Los Alamos was a world unto itself, an island in the sky." As a top-secret army base, it was guarded by armed sentries and surrounded by a barbed-wire fence, albeit one with a hole in it (Native Americans from the nearby pueblos regularly slipped through on their way to the PX). So secret was the work that many of the spouses (overwhelmingly wives) did not know its exact nature. Mail was censored, and there were no personal telephones. Life inside the compound was hard. Substandard housing was a constant nettle. In winter, furnaces would blaze out of control, superheating apartments so that candles melted and walls sizzled. Especially annoying was the absence of bathtubs and bathroom locks in the new and shoddily built housing, which was never intended to outlast the war. The most desirable homes at Los Alamos were on Bathtub Row, a string of prewar houses with real tubs, not just government-issue showers. The eight older houses had rats, but people fought over them anyway. A tub was a sure way to lure a baby-sitter when those were hard to come by, a Los Alamos wife recalled. Water was often in short supply, as were milk, fresh eggs, and fresh vegetables. Dust, on the other hand, was abundant.

Wives bore a greater burden in dealing with these daily difficulties than did their preoccupied husbands. Marshak, wife of theoretical physicist Robert Marshak, who was later president of City College of New York, recalled how it felt to have him disappear every day but Sunday into the post's "holy of holies," the Technical Area, protected by its own barbed-wire fence. As she makes clear, it was the wives who paid the price of their husbands' making history. "The Tech Area," she recalled, "was a great pit which swallowed our scientist husbands out of sight, almost out of our lives. The men were drawn to their work not only by curiosity and zeal, but also by an inspiring patriotism. They worked as they had never worked before. They worked at night and often came home at 3 or 4 in the morning. Sometimes, they set up Army cots in the laboratories and did not come home at all. . . . Few women understood what the men were seeking there or comprehended the magnitude of the search. The loneliness and heartache of some scientists' wives during the years before the atomic bomb was born were very real." It would be wrong to assume causality, but among the lonely was

Kitty Oppenheimer, who began to drink so heavily at Los Alamos that another woman had to take over the laboratory's hostessing duties.

For all the vaunted loneliness of its women, Los Alamos was sexually charged. Jean Bacher, whose husband, Robert, led the Bomb Physics Division and who became a champion of the peaceful uses of atomic energy after the war, described Los Alamos as "peculiarly uninhibited and completely unrelaxed"—an atmosphere that apparently encouraged reproduction. The larger baby boom would have to wait until the war was over, but Los Alamos, where young men engaged in the war effort were not necessarily separated from their spouses, had a baby boomlet of its own. There were eighty births during the first year alone. You knew who the new fathers were. They were the ones standing on packing crates outside the post hospital, looking proudly through the windows into the nursery. Groves was said to be furious about the fecundity of his prima donnas— even the Oppenheimers had a daughter, Katherine, during the project. News that Groves wanted something done about the population boom resulted in a bit of doggerel that was repeated throughout the community:

> The General's in a stew
> He trusted you and you
> He thought you'd be scientific
> Instead you're just prolific
> And what is he to do?

General or no, the babymaking continued unabated.

The role of women in the Manhattan Project is troubling. From Madame Curie, the codiscoverer of polonium and radium, to Lise Meitner, the grievously unsung physicist, who with her nephew, Otto Frisch, first explained how neutron capture could result in the release of enormous amounts of energy, women were crucial at every stage in the history of nuclear physics. But they were a decided minority among the players in the Tech Area. There were a few female physicists and other scientists, but, for the most part, women played supportive roles, doing tedious mathematical calculations, for example, and serving as secretaries. A Rosie-the-Riveter pattern developed at Los Alamos, so that women who might otherwise have stayed home, whatever their gifts and training, did work in the war effort alongside men, but mostly in secondary roles.

Again and again, we have asked ourselves why women weren't present in greater numbers at Los Alamos, PARC, and many other extraordinary collaborations. Clearly, a tragic waste of female talent was tolerated at Los Alamos, as it was virtually everywhere in the Western world before the relatively recent rise of feminism. That this happened even in groups as creative and boundary busting as this one is especially distressing. It is doubly disturbing, given the collaborative nature of these groups. In many ways, women have been the pioneers of collaboration. From Susan B. Anthony and her nineteenth-century sisters who forged the American women's rights movement to Jane Addams and the other women who created such enlightened institutions as the settlement house, women have been in the forefront of identifying our common problems and finding collaborative solutions. And yet, again and again, they have been excluded, or, more properly, marginalized, in some of the most important collaborations of our time.

A tradition of exclusion, no less despicable for being time-honored, is one obvious reason. But we do ourselves a disservice if we don't look beyond that to find other possible reasons as well. Do we educate women differently? (Surely the answer is yes.) Do we continue to have different expectations for men and women vis-á-vis familial obligations—and do men and women continue to have different expectations in these important matters for themselves?

That the women of Los Alamos were courageous is unquestionable. Mici Teller, Edward Teller's wife, organized a highly effective action to keep precious trees from being cut down by army bulldozers. The women simply sat themselves down next to the trees and defied the bulldozers to approach. But few of the women, as remarkable as they were, were able to overcome the lack of cultural support for the notion that they were the equals of the men of the project. Unlike the Percy Bysshe Shelleys of the world, the Mary Shelleys have so much trouble deafening their ears to the hungry baby's cries. Questioned on the matter at a postwar conference, Laura Fermi pointed out that there were women with important roles at Los Alamos. "Mary Argo was a physicist and did have some responsibility in the project," Fermi noted, then added, in a phrase that speaks volumes, "but she had also to take care of her children." Indeed, someone had to.

Despite the hardships of Los Alamos, most of the scientists and others who were there remember it as a time of rare commitment and spirit. Victor Weisskopf, one of the emigré theoreticians, recalled, "You know there was a big fence around us, and we always said, 'That fence doesn't keep us from going out, it keeps others from coming in.' We thought this is a very special place and the people outside should envy us, that we can be here and work at such an important and interesting issue." Weisskopf pointed out that many of the scientists originally hoped that it would be impossible to make the bomb, but once it was clear that it could be built, it was hoped that the result would be the end of all war, not just this war, a notion in which Bohr believed strongly and shared with the others.

Although the morality of the bomb was on the minds of some from the beginning of the project, no one believed the world would be better off if the Germans developed it first. That threat set the frantic pace at Los Alamos. Charlotte Serber, who was the project's scientific librarian, in charge of classified documents as well as other books and papers, said that life in the Tech Area had a "hyperthyroid quality." "Its tempo was too fast; its excitement was almost too high. The Area was in a state of continuous crisis, and it soon became clear that speedup was its permanent tempo and excitement its permanent mood." In that electric atmosphere, ordinary reality could be ignored, for a time. Misgivings about the impact of the bomb could be put on hold. The work sometimes served to distract and deaden the personal pain of participants, including some whose families were trapped in Europe and some, like Feynman, whose young wife was dying of tuberculosis in a hospital in Santa Fe. Although Oppenheimer worked himself to emaciation and exhaustion, he, too, seemed to escape into the work, finding a respite from the suicidal depression that was a dark presence throughout his life.

Although the purpose of the project was high-minded and deadly serious, the atmosphere was not. As always happens in Great Groups, people had enormous amounts of fun. In spite of what some nonscientists think, scientists are not necessarily dour. Oppenheimer was, by nature, a philosophical, rather grave person, but some of his colleagues were anything but. Bethe, who was his right hand, was downright jolly, according to Hirschfelder, who served as a group leader in both the Ordnance and Theoretical Divisions. "My office was down the hall, and I could always tell when Bethe and Feynman were working together because there would be frequent bursts of guffaws and belly laughs." The civilians and their families despised the base's military regulations and mocked them mercilessly. Security was such that the residents were not supposed to refer to anyone as a physicist or a chemist (they were not to call anyone doctor or professor, either). So they called the physicists "fizzlers" and the chemists "stinkers." The atomic bomb itself they called the "Gadget."

For all his genius, Fermi had a decidedly puckish side. His security name was Mr. Farmer, and he is alleged to have approached Niels Bohr, known at Los Alamos as Nicholas Baker or Uncle Nick, after a screening of the film *Madame Curie*: "I've just seen a grand picture," Farmer told Baker. Its title? "*Madame . . . Cooper.*" In an even more pointed joke, Werner Heisenberg was repeatedly paged over the public-address system for two days running. Someone finally told the poor operator that she had been had and that if she wanted Heisenberg she'd have to contact Berlin, where he headed up the German bomb project. Evenings and

Sundays were as hyperthyroid as the long workdays. Square dancing became a rage at Los Alamos, parties were frequent and raucous, and the hospital was kept busy treating ski injuries. Residents discovered the beautiful black pottery made by Maria Martinez at the nearby San Ildefonso pueblo. Kistiakowsky introduced many of the Europeans to the mysteries of poker, making a killing until they got the hang of it.

Los Alamos had no tribal T-shirts, but it did have several distinctive uniforms. In the United States of the early 1940s, women still donned hats and gloves to go to town. But on their island in the sky, women often wore slacks and even jeans, unusual then. Voluminous fiesta skirts, Native American jewelry, and moccasins were also popular. Many of the men wore plaid shirts and jeans or unironed pants, donning ties only when they had their pictures taken. Oppie was known for his porkpie hat. So cohesive and distinctive was the culture of Los Alamos that it could be satirized effectively. Donald Flanders, who led the Computation Group in the Theoretical Division, created a comic ballet called *Sacre du Mesa*. Nicknamed Moll, Flanders also danced the part of General Groves. The main prop, recalled Bernice Brode, who did computations at Los Alamos, "was a mechanical brain with flashing lights and noisy bangs and sputters, which did consistently wrong calculations, for example, $2 + 2 = 5$."

Oppenheimer was the glue that held Los Alamos together. Teller, who would later break so acrimoniously with Oppenheimer, had only the highest praise for his leadership of the wartime lab. "Oppie knew in detail what was going on in every part of the Laboratory," Teller reminisced in 1983. "He was incredibly quick and

perceptive in analyzing human as well as technical problems. . . . He knew how to organize, cajole, humor,
soothe feelings—how to lead powerfully without seem-
ing to do so. He was an exemplar of dedication, a hero
who never lost his humanness. Disappointing him some-
how carried with it a sense of wrongdoing. Los Alamos's
amazing success grew out of the brilliance, enthusiasm
and charisma with which Oppenheimer led it."

It is a tribute to Groves's acumen that he saw the
potential for greatness in Oppenheimer when few others did. Oppenheimer changed at Los Alamos. He
made himself into what was needed. One small but
telling example: At Berkeley, Oppenheimer never
scheduled classes before eleven o'clock in the morning.
At Los Alamos, he was at his desk by 7:30 A.M. Bethe,
whom Oppenheimer chose over Teller to head the
Theoretical Division of the lab, was equally effusive in
Oppenheimer's praise. "He understood immediately
when he heard anything, and fitted it into the general
scheme of things and drew the right conclusions,"
Bethe told Rhodes. "There was just nobody else in that
laboratory who came even close to him. In his knowledge. There was human warmth as well. Everybody
certainly had the impression that Oppenheimer cared
what each particular person was doing. In talking to
someone he made it clear that that person's work was
important for the success of the whole project. I don't
remember any occasion at Los Alamos in which he was
nasty to any person, whereas before and after the war
he was often that way. At Los Alamos he didn't make
anybody feel inferior, not anybody."

Weisskopf talked about Oppenheimer's "continuous
and intense presence, which produced a sense of direct

participation in all of us. It created that unique atmosphere of enthusiasm and challenge that pervaded the place throughout its time." Weisskopf recalled that Oppie had an almost uncanny way of appearing at crucial moments in the complex process. "I remember when I was in a discussion about something important, he sort of showed up. I don't know how he found out we were discussing something important or when an experiment came to the final time when the results would come out, even if it was four o'clock in the morning, he was there."

Some of his colleagues speak of being ennobled by their contact with Oppenheimer. "Oppenheimer stretched me," Wilson said. "His style, the poetic vision of what we were doing, of life, of a relationship to people, inflamed me. In his presence I became more intelligent, more vocal, more intense, more prescient, more poetic myself." Several of his most distinguished fellows talk about the sense of excitement with which he imbued the enterprise. Physicist I. I. Rabi said, "He created an atmosphere of excitement, enthusiasm, and high intellectual and moral purpose that still remains with those who participated as one of the great experiences of their lives." Although some would be disturbed after the war when they learned that Oppenheimer, who was always being grilled by security officers, had been willing to name others active in left-wing causes, during the project his moral leadership was regarded as impeccable. Confidence that the group's leader knew true north was never more important than when the world's most brilliant individuals were asked to build its most apocalyptic weapon.

Oppenheimer was a man of action at Los Alamos as well as a visionary. For all its excitement and camaraderie, Los Alamos was no Camelot. Although the importance of the work kept some interpersonal tensions in check, some became intractable. Oppie had to make painful personnel decisions in order to keep the work going forward. No one was more prickly than Teller, who resisted taking any sort of direction from Bethe. Aware that Teller's genius could not be coerced or cajoled into doing what was most needed, Oppenheimer freed him to work on fusion instead of fission. Oppenheimer realized that there was no other way to guarantee access to Teller's unique gifts.

Another painful decision involved the ongoing tension between Kistiakowsky and Seth Neddermeyer. It was Neddermeyer, a brilliant young physicist, who first proposed the implosion bomb, which would eventually be called Fat Man. Kistiakowsky, the chemist-become-explosives-expert, had come to Los Alamos to administer the implosion work while Neddermeyer continued to work on the science. Kistiakowsky worked well with Deke Parsons, the naval officer in charge of the Ordnance Division. But Neddermeyer and Parsons had been estranged ever since Parsons had sarcastically dismissed Neddermeyer's proposal for an implosion device at a meeting of the staff. By mid-1944, Kistiakowsky was so frustrated by the mistrust shown by Neddermeyer and by the lack of "friendly give-and-take" that he offered to quit. Convinced that Kistiakowsky was too valuable to lose, Oppenheimer decided to put him in charge of the entire implosion project, working under Parsons. Neddermeyer was asked to become a senior technical advisor, a humiliating demotion. Oppenheimer explained, in a letter to Neddermeyer, that he hoped Neddermeyer would be able to accept the new assignment "in behalf of the success of the whole project, as well as the peace of mind and effectiveness of the workers in the H.E. [high explosive] program." As Rhodes recounts, "With enduring bitterness Neddermeyer did." Members of Great Groups sacrifice their egos for the mission. Unselfishness doesn't necessarily eliminate the pain.

You can't help wondering if Oppenheimer would have been quite so universally esteemed, even loved, at Los Alamos if Groves had not been so perfect a lightning rod for its accumulated tensions. Groves was blamed for everything that went wrong, from the age of the eggs in the PX to the work schedules of the Chicana and Native American maids. "He was extremely hard working and efficient, but he had a knack for saying the wrong thing and getting people angry," Hirschfelder recalled. "He never understood the scientists and they thoroughly hated him. For example, when he encouraged his daughter to go into physics, she said to him, 'But, Father, you know what the physicists think of you!' " In Hirschfelder's view, it was Groves's staggering ego that was his undoing. He liked letting people know that Oppenheimer reported to him, for instance. But the elitism of the scientists may have also been a factor in the hard feelings toward Groves, an extraordinary leader who built and administered the project's vast and complex uranium separation operations at Oak Ridge, Tennessee, and atomic piles at Hanford, Washington, in addition to overseeing Los Alamos.

As PARC would be, Los Alamos was a place where people called on each other for advice and even worked on each other's projects. Often people were brought to Los Alamos because of their expertise in one area, solved the assigned problem, and then were turned loose on additional projects for which their only qualification was a world-class mind. (For security reasons, the scientists normally couldn't return to their campuses and labs until the war was over.) Hirschfelder was a classic example. A physicist, he was brought to Los Alamos to determine the characteristics of the gun and gunpowder needed to set off the enriched uranium bomb—Little Boy. He and his colleagues finished the job in three weeks. Next, he was made a group leader in the Theoretical Division, where his group was asked to determine what effects would follow the actual explosion of the bomb. He and his team quickly educated themselves by turning to treatises on aerodynamics, air pollution, and the physics of blown sand. Among their conclusions—one their colleagues resisted until they saw the frightening evidence—the blast would produce radioactive fallout. (As a result of Los Alamos, Hirschfelder came to believe that intellectual flexibility should be an explicit goal of higher education, just as mastery of a discipline is.)

Like other Great Groups, the Manhattan Project tended to look at ability, not credentials, when matching a person to a job. For example, in 1942, plans to separate U-235 from the more common isotope of uranium, U-238, by means of gaseous diffusion were stalled because no satisfactory barrier material for the process existed. One unlikely team assigned the problem consisted of interior decorator Edward Norris, who had developed an electrodeposited nickel mesh for use in an innovative paint sprayer he had designed, and chemist Edward Adler, a favorite student of Nobel Prize winner Harold Urey. The duo came up with a nickel mesh barrier that looked sufficiently promising that a pilot production plant was built (another approach to the problem ultimately won out).

The work at Los Alamos was often hands-on. Kistiakowsky gives a dramatic example. The implosion bomb required perfectly shaped charges. He and his colleagues developed a system for x-raying the explosive castings to uncover flaws caused by air pockets. But they were unable to produce perfect castings. With the pressure of the Trinity test looming, Kistiakowsky worked through the night, using a dentist's drill to reach the air pockets in the flawed castings, then filling the holes with explosives. Kistiakowsky was matter-of-fact about the painstaking, dangerous chore. "You don't worry about it," he told Rhodes. "I mean, if fifty pounds of explosives goes in your lap, you won't know it."

Pragmatism was the gospel of Los Alamos. People often had to improvise, and not just in terms of equipment. People such as Teller, who reacted to every slight and were relentlessly confrontational, often accomplished less than those who found clever, oblique ways to get what they wanted. Kistiakowsky once had a British explosives expert visit the lab. The Englishman thought Kistiakowsky's explosive of choice, Baratol, was inferior to dynamite. Unfortunately, the Englishman was Lord Cherwell, Churchill's top science advisor. Shortly after the visit, Oppenheimer called Kistiakowsky into the office and told him that Roosevelt had received a cable from Churchill saying Baratol wouldn't work. Kistiakowsky recalled suggesting that Oppie tell the sender to go to hell. But Kistiakowsky also did what he had to do and set up a lab to explore the use of dynamite in the implosion project. His instinct might have been to rail impotently against fate. Instead, he found an ingenious way to guarantee that the dynamite work wouldn't interfere with his own Baratol work. He went through the personnel list and chose for the dynamite project only those individuals who had made absolutely no contribution so far. Deliberately staffed with deadwood, the dynamite group was no threat to his own Great Group.

There were those who came to Los Alamos with hopes that the bomb was an impossibility. Those hopes ended forever on July 16, 1945, with the Trinity test, an event Jane Wilson called "the birth of the monster." She was one of the Los Alamos wives who knew something momentous would happen that morning, and she watched from a ski slope in the Jemez mountains. She looked south, toward the test site at Alamogordo. "Five o'clock. Five fifteen. Then it came. The blinding light like no other light one had ever seen. The trees, illuminated, leaping out at one. The mountains flashing into life. Later, the long, slow rumble. Oh, something has happened, all right, for good or for ill. Something wonderful. Something terrible."

The monumental flash caused Oppenheimer to think of a passage from the Bhagavad Gita:

> If the radiance of a thousand suns
> were to burst into the sky,
> that would be like the splendor of the
> Mighty One—

The ominous cloud that followed brought another line to mind, "I am become Death, the shatterer of worlds." Ever the experimentalist, Fermi busied himself dropping pieces of paper in an attempt to determine the strength of the blast. The explosion shifted the paper two and one-half meters, which led Fermi to estimate, correctly, that the bomb released the destructive energy of 10,000 tons of TNT. Most of the scientists were euphoric at the successful test. Bob Wilson (Jane's husband) was not; he told Feynman that they had made a terrible thing. Trinity director Kenneth Bainbridge was somber as well. He congratulated the other scientists, then said to Oppenheimer, "Now we are all sons of bitches." The most chilling words were spoken by Groves. One of his generals approached him and said, "The war is over."

"Yes," Groves responded, "after we drop two bombs on Japan."

At some point in making the bomb, the scientists lost control of it. It was inevitable that they would do so. Bohr, who had come to see the bomb as both an unprecedented horror and an unprecedented opportunity to end war, tried heroically to influence public policy. He met with Roosevelt and Churchill to argue the wisdom of sharing nuclear secrets and developing an international body for the control of nuclear arms. Roosevelt was sympathetic; Churchill was not. Then, the dynamic abruptly shifted. On April 12, 1945, Roosevelt died. The new president, Harry S. Truman, did not learn about Los Alamos and its terrible weapon until he was sworn in. In 1945, it was not only war lovers who argued in favor of using the bomb on the Japanese. The Allies were experiencing horrible casualties in the Pacific. Most people believed that the Japanese would defend their home islands to the death. Experts estimated that hundreds of thousands of Allied soldiers would die in an invasion of Japan. Decent people asked themselves if a demonstration of the bomb would be enough to induce the emperor to surrender. Even Oppenheimer said he wasn't sure.

The *Enola Gay* dropped the first atomic bomb on Hiroshima at 8:15 in the morning of August 6, 1945. Unlike the implosion bomb, the technically simpler Little Boy bomb had never been tested. The men who built it knew it would work. One hundred thousand people died unspeakable deaths in the attack, and thousands more would die from radiation poisoning in the months and years that followed. Fat Man was loosed on Nagasaki on August 9. Japan surrendered five days later.

Truman once told Dean Acheson, his secretary of state, not to bring Oppenheimer to see him again. "After all," Truman said, "all he did was to make the bomb. I'm the guy who fired it off." Truman had none of the qualms that tormented Bohr and others. "Having found the bomb, we have used it," Truman said. "We have used it to shorten the agony of young Americans."

Great Groups always set out to change the world. Few did so as decisively as the Manhattan Project. Many of the people who were at Los Alamos spent lifetimes coming to terms with the implications of their work. What they had done there together had been difficult, thrilling, and enormously important, as no other experience in their lives had been. The Gadget they so zealously created had brought an awful war to an end. But it had also changed the world in ways that raised the most disturbing questions about the uses of science, technology, and human creativity—questions we still grapple with today.

TAKE-HOME
LESSONS

Life in Great Groups is different from much of real life. It's better. *Bambi* veteran Jules Engel recalls that the great Disney animators couldn't wait to get up in the morning to get back to their drawing boards. Fermi and the other geniuses of the Manhattan Project continued to work on the Gadget even when hiking in the mountains on their Sundays off. It wasn't simply that the work was fascinating and vitally important. The process itself was exciting, even joyous. On those rare and happy occasions when you are part of a Great Group, you know the truth of Noel Coward's observation that "work was more fun than fun."

Something happens in these groups that doesn't happen in ordinary ones, even very good ones. Some alchemy takes place that results, not only in a computer revolution or a new art form, but in a qualitative change in the participants. If only for the duration of the project, people in Great Groups seem to become better than themselves. They are able to see more, achieve more, and have a far better time doing it than they can working alone. Groups of the stature of PARC in its glory days and Disney Feature Animation are rare. But they could happen far more often than they do.

Most of us have experienced the terrible frustration of being part of a group that had the potential for greatness but never quite gelled. The geometrical surge in ideas and energy that happens in Great Groups never took place, even though the talent was there, the drive was there, and the project seemed full of promise. Looking back at these stillborn opportunities, you experience a shudder of sadness and inevitably ask yourself, "What went wrong?"

A Great Group is more than a collection of first-rate minds. It is a miracle. But it is a miracle that can't take place unless certain conditions have been met. Some of these are spelled out in an instructive scene in Roland Joffe's 1989 film on the Manhattan Project, *Fat Man and Little Boy*. General Groves, played by Paul Newman, asks Oppenheimer, played by Dwight Schultz, what it will take to get the Gadget built. "Focus," Oppie answers, naming a critical element of every Great Group. "You have all these great minds, but they're all dancing to a different tune. Bring them together in one place. Isolate 'em—no distractions. You create an atmosphere of stress, creative stress, everyone competing to solve one problem. And you have one ringmaster."

As the real-life Oppenheimer so clearly did, the screen Oppie knows his creative collaboration. There is no way to guarantee that any particular group will achieve greatness, but there are ways to maximize the likelihood. Each of the groups we have looked at has important things to teach us, some positive, some cautionary. These are the fifteen top take-home lessons of Great Groups:

1. Greatness starts with superb people. Bob Taylor, the leader of the Great Group at PARC, liked to say, "You can't pile together enough good people to make a great one." He was right. Recruiting the most talented people possible is the first task of anyone who hopes to create a Great Group. The people who can achieve something truly unprecedented have more than enormous talent and intelligence. They have original minds. They see things differently. They can spot the gaps in what we know. They have a knack for discovering interesting, important problems as well as skill in solving them. They want to do the next thing, not the last one. They see connections. Often they have specialized skills, combined with broad interests and multiple frames of reference. They tend to be deep generalists, not narrow specialists. They are not so immersed in one discipline that they can't see solutions in another. They are problem solvers before they are computer scientists or animators. They can no more stop looking for new relationships and new, better ways of doing things than they can stop breathing. And they have the tenacity so important in accomplishing anything of value.

2. Great Groups and great leaders create each other. Great Groups give the lie to the remarkably persistent notion that successful institutions are the lengthened shadow of a great woman or man. It's not clear that life was ever so simple that individuals, acting alone, solved most significant problems. Our tendency to create heroes rarely jibes with the reality that most nontrivial problems require collective solutions. Edison worked hard at maintaining the illusion that his inventions had sprung fully developed from his fecund brain, but he had many collaborators, albeit unsung ones. In our constantly changing, global, highly technological society, collaboration is a necessity. The Lone Ranger, the incarnation of the individual problem solver, is dead. In his place, we have a new model for creative achievement: the Great Group. Great Groups don't exist without great leaders, but they are much more than lengthened shadows of them. Disney, John Andrew Rice, and Steve Jobs not only headed Great Groups, they found their own greatness in them. As Howard Gardner points out, Oppenheimer showed no great administrative ability before or after the Manhattan Project. And yet when the world needed him, he was able to rally inner resources that probably surprised even himself. Inevitably, the leader of a Great Group has to invent a leadership style that suits it. The standard models, especially the command-and-control style, simply won't work. The heads of Great Groups have to act decisively, but never arbitrarily. They have to make decisions without limiting the perceived autonomy of the other participants. Devising and maintaining an atmosphere in which others can put a dent in the universe is the leader's creative act.

3. Every Great Group has a strong leader. This is one of the paradoxes of creative collaboration. Great Groups are made up of people with rare gifts working together as equals. Yet, in virtually every one there is one person who acts as maestro, organizing the genius of the others. He or she is a pragmatic dreamer, a person with an original but attainable vision. Ironically, the leader is able to realize his or her dream only if the others are free to do exceptional work. Typically, the leader is the one who recruits the others, by making the vision so palpable and seductive that they see it, too, and eagerly sign up.

Within the group, the leader is often a good steward, keeping the others focused, eliminating distractions, keeping hope alive in the face of setbacks and stress. One of the simple pleasures of Great Groups is that they are almost never bureaucratic. People in them feel liberated from the trivial and the arbitrary. Often, everyone deals directly with the leader, who can make most decisions on the spot.

Leaders of Great Groups inevitably have exquisite taste. They are not creators in the same sense that the others are. Rather, they are curators, whose job is not to make, but to choose. The ability to recognize excellence in others and their work may be the defining talent of leaders of Great Groups. Oppenheimer couldn't do the individual tasks required to make the bomb, but he knew who could and he was able to sort through alternative solutions and implement the optimal one. Such leaders are like great conductors. They may not be able to play Mozart's First Violin Concerto, but they have a profound understanding of the work and can create the environment needed to realize it.

The leader has to be worthy of the group. He or she must warrant the respect of people who may have greater genius, as Bob Taylor did at PARC. The respect issue is a critical one. Great Groups are voluntary associations. People are in them, not for money, not even for glory, but because they love the work, they love the project. Everyone must have complete faith in the leader's instincts and integrity vis-à-vis the work. Great Groups don't require their leaders to be saints. But they do expect them to be absolutely trustworthy where the project is concerned. Kelly Johnson was a curmudgeon, but he was revered at the Skunk Works for his refusal to compromise about airplanes. On one occasion he returned millions of dollars rather than continue a project he didn't believe in. Walt Disney was an irritable, often small-minded, man, but the people who made his classic animated films knew that his creative choices were almost always impeccable.

4. The leaders of Great Groups love talent and know where to find it. Great Groups are headed by people confident enough to recruit people better than themselves. They revel in the talent of others.

Where do you find people good enough to form a Great Group? Sometimes they find you. The talented smell out places that are full of promise and energy, the places where the future is being made. The gifted often catch the zeitgeist and ride it to a common shore. Certain schools and academic departments are lodestones for talent. Certain cities attract it as well. All roads lead to Seattle for many computer programmers and for the best rock musicians of a certain style. Cyberspace has also become a place where talented people gather, liberated from geography.

Word of mouth can draw new talent to a Great Group, as it did at Black Mountain. But the quality of a group often reflects the network of its leader. Many Great Groups start with great Rolodexes. Oppenheimer knew the physicists he wanted for the Manhattan Project because he was part of an international community of physicists who had trained at the best schools and kept abreast of each other's work through scientific journals and international conferences. Bob Taylor knew the most gifted computer scientists of his day because he had evaluated their work for federal funding. Charles Olson relied on his wide circle of literary friends when he recruited for Black Mountain.

The broader and more diverse the network, the greater the potential for a Great Group. The richer the mix of people, the more likely that new connections will be made, new ideas will emerge.

Being part of a group of superb people has a profound impact on every member. Participants know that inclusion is a mark of their own excellence. Everyone in such a group becomes engaged in the best kind of competition—a desire to perform as well as or better than one's colleagues, to warrant the esteem of people for whom one has the highest respect. People in Great Groups are always stretching because of the giants around them. For members of such groups, the real competition is with themselves, an ongoing test of just how good they are and how completely they can use their gifts.

5. Great Groups are full of talented people who can work together. This may seem obvious, but talent can be so dazzling, so seductive, that the person who is recruiting may forget that not every genius works well with others. Certain tasks can only be performed collaboratively, and it is madness to recruit people, however gifted, who are incapable of working side by side toward a common goal. Joseph Rotblat, who won the Nobel Peace Prize in 1996 for his lifelong effort to ban nuclear weapons, was the only scientist to quit the Manhattan Project on moral grounds—he was appalled that its scientists agreed to keep their discoveries secret from the Soviets and others. Despite his extraordinary ability as a theoretical physicist, he was utterly unsuited for the Manhattan Project because his strong personal vision was incompatible with that of the group. Those powerful convictions allowed Rotblat to create a remarkable group of his own, the London-based Pugwash Conferences, that reflects his commitment to open science and nuclear disarmament.

Although the ability to work together is a prerequisite for membership in a Great Group, being an amiable person, or even a pleasant one, isn't. Great Groups are probably more tolerant of personal idiosyncrasies than are ordinary ones, if only because the members are so intensely focused on the work itself. That all-important task acts as a social lubricant, minimizing frictions. Sharing information and advancing the work are the only real social obligations.

A good colleague may be defined differently in Great Groups than in ordinary ones. When your mission in life is to find a new way for people to interact with information or some other exalted goal, you may be willing to tolerate social obtuseness in a colleague who helps you do it. People who are engaged in groundbreaking collaborations have high regard for people who challenge and test their ideas. In such a group, ordinary affability may be no virtue. The young Richard Feynman was infamous for telling his older, more famous colleagues at Los Alamos that one or another of their ideas was stupid. But Feynman was valued in the project because the impolitic judgment was routinely followed by a probing question or penetrating insight that boosted the level of everyone's thought. On at least one occasion, Niels Bohr sought Feynman out, because Bohr knew Feynman would candidly evaluate his ideas and not be cowed, as so many others were, by Bohr's towering reputation. Whether Feynman's associates liked him or not, they recognized him as a good colleague: he advanced their common cause.

6. Great Groups think they are on a mission from God. Whether they are trying to get their candidate into the White House or trying to save the free world, Great Groups always believe that they are doing something vital, even holy. They are filled with believers, not doubters, and the metaphors that they use to describe their work are commonly those of war and religion. People in Great Groups often have the zeal of converts, people who have come only recently to see some great truth and follow it wherever it leads.

Great Groups are engaged in holy wars. The psychology of these high-minded missions is clear. People know going in that they will be expected to make sacrifices, but they also know they are doing something monumental, something worthy of their best selves. When you are frantically writing computer code, fueled by Coke and pizza, you don't wonder whether your work is meaningful. You are fully engaged, absorbed by the problem, lost in the task. But people in Great Groups are different from those who spend countless hours in thrall to video games or other trivial pursuits. Their clear, collective purpose makes everything they do seem meaningful and valuable.

A powerful enough vision can transform what would otherwise be loss and drudgery into sacrifice. The scientists of the Manhattan Project were willing to put their careers on hold and to undertake what was, in essence, a massive engineering feat because they believed the free world depended on their doing so. Reminiscing about Los Alamos, Feynman told a story that illustrates how effectively the vision can give meaning and value to work. The army had recruited talented engineers and others from all over the United States for special duty on the project. They were assigned to work on the primitive computers of the period, doing energy calculations and other tedious jobs. But the army, obsessed with security, refused to tell them anything specific about the project. They didn't know that they were building a weapon that could end the war or even what their calculations meant. They were simply expected to do the work, which they did—slowly and not very well. Feynman, who supervised the technicians, prevailed on his superiors to tell the recruits what they were doing and why. Permission was granted to lift the veil of secrecy, and Oppenheimer gave them a special lecture on the nature of the project and their own contribution.

"*Complete* transformation," Feynman recalled. "*They* began to invent ways of doing it better. They improved the scheme. They worked at night. They didn't need supervising in the night; they didn't need anything. They understood everything; they invented several of the programs that we used." Ever the scientist, Feynman calculated that the work was done "nearly ten times as fast" after it had meaning.

Able leaders inspire groups engaged in less momentous projects as well. James Carville was particularly adept at keeping the staff and volunteers in the 1992 Clinton War Room fired up. Like Steve Jobs at Apple, he had a gift for finding the language that made hard work seem both purposeful and fun. CEO Herb Kelleher makes fun a priority at innovative and wildly successful Southwest Airlines. But he has also persuaded his team that the airline has an exalted mission. Southwest doesn't simply provide customers with cheap flights from Dallas to Tucson. It offers passengers something far more precious—the "freedom of travel." Leaders of Great Groups understand the power of rhetoric. They recruit people for crusades, not jobs.

7. Every Great Group is an island—but an island with a bridge to the mainland. Great Groups become their own worlds. They also tend to be physically removed from the world around them. Los Alamos was located in the high desert miles from Santa Fe and was surrounded by a barbed-wire fence. The Skunk Works operated as an independent community within Lockheed, its secret activities conducted behind unmarked doors. People who are trying to change the world need to be isolated from it, free from its distractions, but still able to tap its resources. Great Groups aren't cloisters. As people so often do in isolated communities, participants in Great Groups create a culture of their own— with distinctive customs, dress, jokes, even a private language. They find their own names for the things that are important to them, a language that both binds them together and keeps nonmembers out. Such groups tend to treasure their secrets.

People in Great Groups also have a great deal of fun. The intensity sometimes becomes giddiness. *Fortune* magazine caught the goofy quality at Netobjects, a software start-up in Redwood City, California, where the staff was racing against deadline to produce a superior web-site designer. Crowded into cubicles, the team never left the building for lunch or dinner but occasionally broke for morning Ping-Pong. They also sported fanciful balloon hats, given to each new staffer on his or her first day. Great Groups are not only fun, they are sexy. There is often an erotic element to working together so closely and intensely. In the charged atmosphere of these groups, people sometimes look across a crowded lab or cubicle and see more than a colleague.

8. Great groups see themselves as winning underdogs. They inevitably view themselves as the feisty David, hurling fresh ideas at a big, backward-looking Goliath. Much of the gleeful energy of Great Groups seems to stem from this view of themselves as upstarts who will snatch the prize from the fumbling hands of a bigger but less wily competitor. In marketing the Macintosh, which Steve Jobs did so brilliantly, he always contrasted his spunky little band of Mac makers with the staid industry giant, IBM. The Mac, he made clear, wasn't your father's computer. In 1992, the Clinton campaign staff successfully presented its candidate as a fresh alternative to the government-as-usual of George Bush. The fact that Bush was the incumbent, the insider, the representative of the Establishment gave added energy to Clinton's campaign.

9. Great Groups always have an enemy. Sometimes, of course, they really do have an enemy, as the scientists of the Manhattan Project had in the Axis powers. But when there is no enemy, you have to make one up. Why? Because, as Coca-Cola CEO Roberto Goizueta has pointed out, you can't have a war without one. Whether the enemy occurs in nature or is manufactured, it serves the same purpose. It raises the stakes of the competition, it helps your group rally and define itself (as everything the enemy is not), and it also frees you to be spurred by that time-honored motivator—self-righteous hatred. Today, Microsoft billionaire William Gates is the face on the dartboard of every computer start-up. Research by social psychologist Teresa M. Amabile and others confirms Goizueta's wisdom. Competition with an outsider seems to boost creativity. "Win-lose" competition within the group reduces it.

10. People in Great Groups have blinders on. The project is all they see. In Great Groups, you don't find people who are distracted by peripheral concerns, including such perfectly laudable ones as professional advancement and the quality of their private lives. Ivy League colleges are full of well-rounded people. Great Groups aren't. Great Groups are full of indefatigable people who are struggling to turn a vision into a machine and whose lawns and goldfish have died of neglect. Such people don't stay up nights wondering if they are spending enough time with the children. For the duration, participants have only one passion—the task at hand. People in Great Groups fall in love with the project. They are so taken with the beauty and difficulty of the task that they don't want to talk about anything else, be anywhere else, do anything else. In the course of joining the group, such people never ask, "How much does it pay?" They ask, "How soon can I start?" and "When can I do it again?" But Great

Groups often have a dark side. Members frequently make a Faustian bargain, trading the quiet pleasures of normal life for the thrill of discovery. Their families often pay the price. For some group members, the frenzied labor of the project is their drug of choice, a way to evade other responsibilities or to deaden loss or pain.

11. Great Groups are optimistic, not realistic. People in Great Groups believe they can do things no one has ever done before. The term for that isn't realism. Such groups are often youthful, filled with talented people who have not yet bumped up against their limits or other dispiriting life lessons. They don't yet know what they can't do. Indeed, they're not sure the impossible exists. According to psychologist Martin Seligman, depressed people tend to be more realistic than optimistic ones. And the optimists, even when their good cheer is unwarranted, accomplish more. They do better in school, for example. As Seligman explained to *Fortune* magazine, the people most likely to succeed are those who combine "reasonable talent with the ability to keep going in the face of defeat." In a study Seligman did for insurance giant Met Life, he found that optimistic salespeople outsold their pessimistic colleagues by more than a third and that optimism was a better predictor of productivity than any of the company's standard measures. If optimism is a major factor in selling insurance, it is even more important when people are attempting to do extraordinarily difficult things under pressure. Great things are accomplished by talented people who believe they will accomplish them. (Henry Ford, or one of his ghostwriters, put it nicely: "If you think you can't, you're right. And if you think you can, you're right.") People in Great Groups are simultaneously analytical and confident. As Alan Kay once observed, "The way to do good science is to be incredibly critical without being depressed." Great Groups don't lose hope in the face of complexity. The difficulty of the task adds to their joy.

12. In Great Groups the right person has the right job. This, too, may seem obvious, but the failure to find the right niche for people—or to let them find their own perfect niches—is a major reason that so many workplaces are mediocre, even toxic, in spite of the presence of talent.

Too many companies believe people are interchangeable. Truly gifted people never are. They have unique talents. Such people cannot be forced into roles they are not suited for, nor should they be. Effective leaders allow great people to do the work they were born to do. Despite the terrible pressure to finish Little Boy and Fat Man, Oppenheimer let Edward Teller drop a vital computational project to pursue a personal line of research that would eventually lead to the hydrogen bomb but had little impact on the urgent work at hand. Oppenheimer reasoned that a happier Teller would make a greater contribution than a disgruntled one to the intellectual life of the community.

Many projects never transcend mediocrity because their leaders suffer from the Hollywood syndrome. This is the arrogant and misguided belief that power is more important than talent. It is the too common view that everyone should be so grateful for a role in a picture or any other job that he or she should be willing to do whatever is asked, even if it's dull or demeaning (at this point in the casting process the starlet is told about the nude scene). When the person and the task are properly matched, the work can proceed with passion. Great Groups allow participants to find their workplace bliss. No steward of a Great Group ever felt, as Xerox executive Bob Sparacino apparently did, that "People shouldn't work because they love it. They should work because it hurts." Talented people working because it hurts is a formula for organizational disaster.

13. The leaders of Great Groups give them what they need and free them from the rest. Successful groups reflect the leader's profound, not necessarily conscious, understanding of what brilliant people want. Most of all, they want a worthy challenge, a task that allows them to explore the whole continent of their talent. They want colleagues who stimulate and challenge them and whom they can admire. What they don't want are trivial duties and obligations. Successful leaders strip the workplace of nonessentials. Great Groups are never places where memos are the primary form of communication. They aren't places where anything is filed in triplicate. Time that can go into thinking and making is never wasted on activities, such as writing reports, that serve only some bureaucratic or corporate function outside the group.

As one Great Group after another has shown, talented people don't need fancy facilities. It sometimes seems that any old garage will do. But they do need the right tools. The leaders of PARC threatened to quit if the lab was not allowed to build the computer it needed, rather than accept an inferior technology. Cutting-edge technology is often a key element in creative collaboration. The right tools become part of the creative process.

All Great Groups share information effectively. Many of the leaders we have looked at were brilliant at ensuring that all members of the group had the information they needed. Bob Taylor's weekly meeting at PARC was a simple, efficient mechanism for sharing data and ideas. Oppenheimer overcame the strong objections of the army to ensure that all his scientists were able to share any and all information with each other. He, too, had weekly colloquia. The impulse behind this openness wasn't solely a democratic one. Great Groups require ideas—the more the better. One idea sparks another. One individual in the group may have the insight or data that causes another's half-idea to click.

Great Groups also tend to be places without dress codes, set hours, or other arbitrary regulations. The freedom to work when you are moved to, wearing what you want, is one that everyone treasures. The casual dress so typical of people in extraordinary groups may be symbolic as well, a sign that they are unconventional thinkers, engaged in something revolutionary. Jeans and a T-shirt have become a uniform for people in innovative groups. Wearing a suit and tie to an interview at a hot start-up company is as sure a way to guarantee not being hired as wearing shorts to an interview at IBM.

One thing Great Groups do need is protection. Great Groups do things that haven't been done before. Most corporations and other traditional organizations say they want innovation, but they reflexively shun the untried. Most would rather repeat a past success than gamble on a new idea. Because Great Groups break new ground, they are more susceptible than others to being misunderstood, resented, even feared. Successful leaders find ways to insulate their people from bureaucratic meddling. They keep the "suits" and other conventional thinkers at a distance, allowing the group to work undistracted. General Groves was a master at this. At Lockheed, Kelly Johnson joined the board of directors to better represent the interests of the Skunk Works. The steward of a Great Group also has to make the case for its product or project within the organization if it is to see the light of day. The leaders at PARC, so able in other ways, failed to convince Xerox to manufacture the group's pioneering personal computer. Steve Jobs didn't have an original paradigm for the Macintosh, but he did get it built and shipped.

One vital function of the leaders of Great Groups is to keep the stress in check. Innovative places are exhilarating, but they are also incubators for massive coronaries. Sundays off helped at Los Alamos and the Skunk Works. Interpersonal stress is trickier. Because Great Groups are obsessed with the project at hand, they are probably less given to rivalry and intrigue than most. Ideally, they are filled with people whose behavior reflects their mutual respect and regard. That's not always the case. In the Clinton War Room, James Carville could be as nasty and peremptory as any drill sergeant. But civility is the preferred social climate for creative collaboration. In an era of downsizing and underemployment, many workplaces have become angry, anguished, poisonous places where managers are abusive and employees subvert each other. Such an environment isn't just morally offensive. It is a bad place to do good work.

Genuine camaraderie, based on shooting the moon together, is the ideal climate of a Great Group. When less attractive emotions come to the fore, they have to be dealt with before they threaten the project. Taylor's model for resolving conflicts, which encourages colleagues to understand each other's positions, even if they disagree, is an especially useful one.

Members of Great Groups also need relative autonomy, a sine qua non of creativity. No Great Group was ever micromanaged. In such groups, it is understood that the talent has to be unleashed to find its own unique solutions to problems it alone can see. Disney could imagine a great character and knew one when he saw one, but he could never animate one to his own high standard. His animators held the secrets of making a Disney character come to life. Leaders of Great Groups trade the illusion of control that micromanaging gives for the higher satisfactions of orchestrating extraordinary achievement.

14. Great Groups ship. Successful collaborations are dreams with deadlines. They are places of action, not think tanks or retreat centers devoted solely to the generation of ideas. Great Groups don't just talk about things (although they often do that at considerable length). They make things—amazing, original things, such as a plane that a bat can't find. Great Groups are hands-on. Think of Kistiakowsky, the great chemist, sitting with a dentist's drill correcting defects in castings because that was what the project needed. The thing being made has many uses within the group. It incarnates the dream, but it is something real, distinct from the people who are creating it, yet shaped by their hands. The thing, the task, is what brings the group together and keeps it grounded and focused. Although the members of the group may love the creative process, they know it has to end. By definition, Great Groups continue to struggle until the project is brought to a successful conclusion. They don't quit until the new computer is out the door with their names on it, as Tom West liked to say. Great curiosity and problem-solving ability are not enough. There must also be continuous focus on the task until the work is done, the rebel computer created and delivered. As Steve Jobs so often reminded his team, "Real artists ship."

15. Great work is its own reward. Great Groups are engaged in solving hard, meaningful problems. Paradoxically, that process is difficult but exhilarating as well. Some primal human urge to explore and discover, to see new relationships and turn them into wonderful new things drives these groups. The payoff is not money, or even glory. Again and again, members of Great Groups say they would have done the work for nothing. The reward is the creative process itself. Problem solving douses the human brain with chemicals that make us feel good. People look back on PARC or the Clinton War Room, and they recall how wonderful it was to work that hard and that well. There is a lesson here that could transform our anguished workplaces overnight. People ache to do good work. Given a task they believe in and a chance to do it well, they will work tirelessly for no more reward than the one they give themselves.

People who have been in Great Groups never forget them, although most groups do not last very long. Our suspicion is that such collaborations have a certain half-life, that, if only because of their intensity, they cannot be sustained indefinitely. Since creative collaboration is done by intellectual explorers, it is not surprising that most Great Groups are temporary. They ship, and soon end. Although Los Alamos takes up enormous psychic space in the memories of those who were there, that phase of the Manhattan Project lasted less than thirty-six months.

Why do these fertile associations end? Perhaps the members reach the ever-so-dispiriting age of reason (30? 40?) and suddenly realize that not everything is possible. Or perhaps the paradigm shifts and what was once a thrilling cluster of ideas is suddenly ossified into orthodoxy.

But a few Great Groups survive for enviable periods. Disney Animation has managed to reinvent itself in recent years by combining Walt Disney's way of engaging the Inner Child with the business acumen of a new generation of Disney executives. And even when Great Groups succumb, some fortunate participants find new ways to get the endorphins flowing. Steve Jobs experienced the extraordinary highs of both the Mac team and Pixar, the studio that made the first wholly computerized animated feature, *Toy Story*. Bob Taylor helped invent the Internet as well as the user-friendly computer.

Creative collaboration is so powerful a phenomenon that it inevitably raises moral issues. As we looked at one Great Group after another, we kept coming back to what we began to call the Wannsee question. Wannsee, of course, was the suburb of Berlin where Hitler's minions gathered in 1942 and formulated the plan for the murder of the world's Jews. The question: Can creative collaboration take place in an evil cause? The answer is yes. The men at Wannsee were no geniuses, but, united by a single, evil vision, using cutting-edge technology and working with missionary zeal, they nearly destroyed an entire people in just three years. As long as talent can be recruited for immoral causes (and there may be an element of emotional intelligence that limits that, Heisenberg notwithstanding), terrible new things can be invented, wreaking havoc on an undreamed-of scale.

Whether you are part of a group that is developing a cure for cancer or one that is creating a weapon that could destroy the human race, the intense pleasures of creative collaboration can cause a kind of moral paralysis. Great Groups are so exciting, so absorbing that it is possible, while caught up in them, even to forget issues of right and wrong. Too often, talented people pour all their intelligence and energy into an unworthy task—the development in the 1950s of the asbestos-packed Micronite filter for Kent cigarettes is a case in point. Great Groups are roller-coaster rides, and all that emotion can keep participants from scrutinizing the content of a project, something we ignore with dangerous regularity.

Feynman tells a cautionary tale about Los Alamos in the minutes after the Trinity-test bomb exploded and changed the world forever.

"There was tremendous excitement," he recalled. "Everybody had parties, we all ran around. I sat on the end of the jeep and beat drums." There was only one person, Bob Wilson, who sat by himself, looking serious and sad. Feynman asked Wilson why he was so glum. "It's a terrible thing that we made," Wilson answered. "But you started it," Feynman said. "You got us into it." And suddenly Feynman understood what had happened to all these great thinkers, caught up in the frenzy of their collective work. "What happened to me," he would later explain, "what happened to the rest of us—is we *started* for a good reason, then you're working very hard to accomplish something and it's a pleasure, it's excitement. And you stop thinking, you know, you just *stop*."

Even in a Great Group, you can't think so hard that you forget to think.

SOURCE NOTES

The End of the Great Man

As always happens in creative collaboration, many sources helped shape our thinking. John Briggs's classic *Fire in the Crucible* (New York: St. Martin's, 1988), which includes the material on Pilobolus, is an especially well-written and provocative examination of the subject. Harold J. Leavitt and Jean Lipman-Blumen's "Hot Groups" (*Harvard Business Review*, July 1995) is as insightful as it is wonderfully written. Howard Gardner's *Leading Minds: An Anatomy of Leadership* (New York: Basic Books, 1995) was especially helpful in its analysis of Oppenheimer's leadership of the Manhattan Project. Psychologist Martin E. P. Seligman did groundbreaking work on optimism and success. We often consulted his classic *Learned Optimism* (New York: Knopf, 1991). (Additional Seligman material is from Alan Farnham's "Are You Smart Enough to Keep Your Job?" in *Fortune,* January 15, 1996). Howard S. Becker's *Art Worlds* (Berkeley: University of California Press, 1982) is a wonderful examination of artistic creativity. Social psychologist Teresa M. Amabile has studied creativity rigorously for twenty years. Her *Creativity in Context* (Boulder, Co.: Westview Press, 1996) was especially helpful in summing up the current science relevant to organizing genius. No one was more helpful than Michael P. Farrell. His "Artists' Circles and the Development of Artists" (in *Small Group Behavior,*

November 1982) was an important source, as was a portion of his book, *Collaborative Friendship Circles, Creative Work, and Adult Development,* that he shared with us prior to publication. We also found much to think about in John A. Byrne's *The Whiz Kids* (New York: Currency, 1993). *Groups That Work (and Those That Don't),* edited by J. Richard Hackman (San Francisco: Jossey-Bass, 1990) was also stimulating. Phil Jackson's observation about Dennis Rodman appeared in the *New York Times Magazine* in Jeff Coplon's piece on the Chicago Bulls, "Legends. Champions?" (April 21, 1996). The Michael Eisner material is from a speech he gave to the Chicago Executives Club at the Chicago Hilton on April 19, 1996. Robert Boyle recalled Hitchcock in an interview in 1996. John Dash retells the story of the Women's Factory Strike in *We Shall Not Be Moved* (New York: Scholastic, 1996). Martinez talked about recruiting in "What Exactly Is Charisma?" by Patricia Sellers in *Fortune,* January 15, 1996 (also the source of the Orit Gadiesh observation on "true north"). Christopher Darden wrote about Marcia Clark in "Marcia and Me" in *Newsweek* (March 25, 1996). Welch summed up his leadership responsibilities in "Where Leaders Come From" in *Fortune,* September 19, 1994. Neil Baldwin's fine biography, *Edison: Inventing the Century* (New York: Hyperion, 1995) was the source for the material on how the inventor recruited. Licklider's enthusiasm for the Miller Analogies Test is revealed, as part of the story of the birth of the Internet, in *When Wizards Stay Up Late: The Origins of the Internet* (New York: Simon & Schuster, 1996) by Katie Hafner and Matthew Lyon. Conversations with Richard Massimilian also contributed.

Troupe Disney

Peter Schneider, head of Feature Animation at Disney throughout its recent renaissance, answered our many questions on how the department is currently organized to maximize creativity but still get the movies shipped on time. We are grateful for his candor, his insights, and his help. Walt Disney is much written about. For biographical information, we found Leonard Mosley's *Disney's World* (Lanham, Md.: Scarborough House, 1990) full of revealing anecdotes and less fawning than some. We also found useful material in *The Man Behind the Magic: The Story of Walt Disney* by Katherine and Richard Greene (New York: Viking, 1991). One of the best sources for detailed information on the making of *Snow White and the Seven Dwarfs* is John Grant's *Encyclopedia of Walt Disney's Animated Characters* (New York: Hyperion, 1993), a must-have book for anyone interested in the animated features. Leonard Maltin has a fine chapter on Disney (the source of the Shamus Culhane material, among other things) in his excellent *Of Mice and Magic: A History of American Animated Cartoons* (New York: Plume, 1987). Film historian Rudy Behlmer also has a fact-packed chapter on *Snow White* in his *America's Favorite Movies: Behind the Scenes* (New York: Frederic Unger, 1982). (Instead of recycling Hollywood legends, Behlmer dug up the studio memos that document the production). Another very useful source was a somewhat eccentric collection of essays titled *Disney Discourse: Producing the Magic Kingdom* (New York and London: Routledge, 1994). Paul Hollister's wonderful portrait of the studio during the making of *Fantasia,* which originally appeared in the *Atlantic Monthly* in December 1940, is in the book.

Other first-rate pieces in the collection are Richard deCordova's "The Mickey in Macy's Window: Childhood, Consumerism, and Disney Animation"; Robert De Roos's "The Magic Worlds of Walt Disney," which originally appeared in *National Geographic* in August 1963 and is the source of the bee story; Richard Neupert's "Painting a Plausible World: Disney's Color Prototypes"; Douglas Gomery's "Disney's Business History: A Reinterpretation"; and Jon Lewis's "Disney after Disney: Family Business and the Business of Family." Disney routinely publishes lavishly illustrated books in connection with new animated features. One we found very useful is by Disney biographer Bob Thomas: *Disney's Art of Animation: From Mickey Mouse to Beauty and the Beast* (New York: Hyperion, 1991). We also found much material in Disney's *Aladdin: The Making of an Animated Film* (New York: Hyperion, 1992). Written by John Culhane, nephew of the great Disney animator Shamus Culhane, it walks the reader through the many stages of production. Much of the information on Andreas Deja comes from Betsy Sharkey's revealing portrait, "The Heart and Soul of a New Animator," in the *New York Times,* May 19, 1996. James Bates and Patrice Apodaca did a first-rate analysis of the rising fortunes of today's animators and the threat posed to Disney by the proliferation of new studios, "Stalking the King of Animation," in the *Los Angeles Times* on June 20, 1996. Burr Snider profiled John Lasseter and Pixar in "The Toy Story Story," in the December 1995 issue of *Wired.* We were also fortunate in being able to turn to Disney founding archivist Dave Smith with questions. He identified the studio's first woman animator for us. He is also the author of the last word on all things Disney, *Disney A to Z: The Official Encyclopedia* (New York: Hyperion, 1996).

A Computer with a Rebel Heart

We were very fortunate to interview Alan Kay, one of the key participants in the creation of the personal computer. He generously shared his insights on how Bob Taylor so effectively organized the talent at Xerox PARC, and, as we talked, we had a sense of how thrilling it must have been to be involved with people of Kay's quality of mind, inventing something that changed the world. Several secondary sources were also invaluable. The first was *Fumbling the Future: How Xerox Invented, Then Ignored the First Personal Computer* by Douglas K. Smith and Robert C. Alexander (New York: William Morrow, 1988). Few books do such a fine job of telling complicated and intertwined stories, in this case, the twisted tales of a triumphant intellectual journey and a corporate fiasco. The book is filled with examples of how to facilitate creative collaboration (Taylor's conflict-resolution technique, for instance) and how to squelch it. Another treasure was Steven Levy's *Insanely Great: The Life and Times of Macintosh, the Computer That Changed Everything* (New York: Viking, 1994). Levy's is a great book, written with a novelist's skill (on a Macintosh, of course). Like the Mac itself, it is an elegant product as well, handsomely produced in an easy-to-hold small format. Levy demystifies the technical part of the computing story and remembers to include the jokes ("What's the difference between Apple and Boy Scouts?"). Another great help was Robert X. Cringely's breezily written but information-laden *Accidental Empires: How the Boys of Silicon Valley Make Their Millions,*

Battle Foreign Competition, and Still Can't Get a Date
(Reading, Mass.: Addison-Wesley, 1992). Cringely, who
proudly calls himself a computer-industry gossip colum-
nist, is awfully good at limning the personalities behind
the millions, but he also writes clearly and amusingly
about ideas. We also watched his three-hour video version of the book, which aired on PBS in 1996, *Triumph
of the Nerds* (from Ambrose Video). Dennis Shasha and
Cathy Lazere's *Out of Their Minds* (New York: Coperni-
cus, 1995) was also invaluable. Gary Wolf's interview
with Steve Jobs in *Wired* magazine (February 1996) is a
fascinating look at the current thinking of this major figure in the evolving story of the personal computer. Also
helpful was Laurence Zuckerman's updated profile of
Mac artist Susan Kare in the *New York Times* (August 26,
1996). Lloyd Krieger's tribute to the Macs he has known
and loved ran in the *New York Times* (February 18,
1996). The Gates-Jobs anecdote is from *Gates* by Stephen
Manes and Paul Andrews (New York: Doubleday, 1994).

Selling a Place Called Hope

Virtually anything you want to know about the 1992
presidential election is contained in *The Quest for the
Presidency 1992,* an exhaustive and compelling example
of journalism as history in the making by Peter Goldman, Thomas M. DeFrank, Mark Miller, Andrew
Murr, and Tom Mathews, with Patrick Rogers and
Melanie Cooper (College Station: Texas A & M University Press, 1994). This team from *Newsweek* had rare
behind-the-scenes access to the Clinton campaign, and
they flesh out their massive account with documents as
well as vividly written scenes of every stage of the process that led to Clinton's election in 1992. We found it

invaluable. The same team was responsible for another good source, the special election issue of *Newsweek* (November/December 1992). In some ways that special issue, released only days after Clinton's win, is even more impressive than the book—an example of journalistic grace under deadline pressure. Another indispensable source was *All's Fair: Love, War, and Running for President* (New York: Random House, 1994). Cowritten by political odd couple Mary Matalin and James Carville, with Peter Knobler, this is an insider's account of the race from both sides. Since our focus was mostly on the Clinton side of the campaign, we found Carville's material especially helpful. The Ragin' Cajun starred in another important source, *The War Room*, Chris Hegedus and D.A. Pennebaker's 1993 Oscar-winning documentary film about the campaign. It is wonderful to be able to see the visuals as this Great Group coalesces, labors mightily, and then suddenly finds its work over. We were also helped enormously in bringing the chapter up to date by an interview with Presidential aide John Emerson in 1996. He was especially helpful in making us appreciate how many people played important roles in the campaign effort—a useful corrective to the somewhat narrow focus of the film. Throughout the 1996 campaign, as Dick Morris rose and fell and as Bob Dole struggled heroically against widespread indifference to his candidacy, we followed the coverage of the *Wall Street Journal*, the *New York Times*, the *Los Angeles Times*, other major papers, and *Time* and *Newsweek*, among other periodicals. Doyle McManus's cover story, "Into the Final Fray," on the emergence of a new, more conservative Clinton in the *Los Angeles Times Magazine* of February 11, 1996, was especially illuminating. Also helpful was Alison Mitchell's peek into the White House campaign center in the *New York Times,* May 7, 1996. We also read the campaign novel *Primary Colors* (New York: Random House, 1996), and, no, we didn't recognize Joe Klein as Anonymous.

The Skunk Works

Given our focus, the best book on Lockheed's super-secret division is *Skunk Works: A Personal Memoir of My Years at Lockheed* by its late head Ben R. Rich and writer Leo Janos (Boston: Little, Brown, 1994). We relied on it both for its admirably lucid descriptions of the complex projects undertaken there and for what Rich and others had to say about their tenure. Rich did an especially good job of contrasting his leadership style with that of his predecessor. Also enormously useful was *Kelly: More Than My Share of It* by the department's legendary founder Clarence L. "Kelly" Johnson, with Maggie Smith (Washington, D.C.: Smithsonian Institution Press, 1985). Kelly's book was written when much about Skunk Works' projects was still classified, but it does an excellent job of describing complex work in accessible language. It also captures both Kelly's crustiness and the pain of his last years. We were also fortunate to have an extensive interview on the Skunk Works with Chris Karen, former head of research at Lockheed. H. S. "Blackie" Shanlian's description of how Johnson recruited is from Tom Peters's *A Passion for Excellence* (New York: Random House, 1985).

Experiment at Black Mountain

In 1972, Martin Duberman's pioneering *Black Mountain: An Exploration in Community* (New York:

E. P. Dutton, 1972) brought the extraordinary school to the attention of a new generation of social and sensory explorers who could appreciate its pioneering spirit—its vibe—and mourn its passing. Duberman not only collected and analyzed prodigious amounts of information, he wrote a courageous, personal book about the process of writing history. We admired it when it came out, and we found it invaluable in writing this book. Another major source was Mary Emma Harris's *The Arts at Black Mountain College* (Cambridge, Mass.: MIT Press, 1987). This, too, is a wonderful book, full of much new material, meticulously documented, and lavishly illustrated. Black Mountain ran on talk, and it is no surprise that many who were associated with it have written compelling reminiscences. Mervyn Lane collected many of these in *Black Mountain College: Sprouted Seeds: An Anthology of Personal Accounts* (Knoxville: University of Tennessee Press, 1990). Thanks to Lane, we had access to the memories and voices of several dozen Black Mountaineers. People continue to remember Black Mountain, gone since 1956. We found much rich material, including candid recollections and wonderful photos, in the special Black Mountain College Issue of the *North Carolina Literary Review* (vol. II, no. 2, 1995). Archivist Shonnie Finnegan kindly answered questions about Olson. We were also most fortunate to have been given a tour of both Black Mountain's former campuses by Mary Holden, a resident of the tiny town of the same name and founder of the Black Mountain Museum and Arts Center. Holden found us, strangers, on her doorstep one Sunday morning in 1996 and took time out from making biscuits and taking children to dance class to show us the places where Rice, Albers, and Olson had defied educational convention. She generously shared her knowledge of the college's cast of characters, including her memories of the Black Mountain reunion that she organized in 1995.

The Manhattan Project

Even Oppenheimer probably didn't know as much about the Manhattan Project as Richard Rhodes does. Rhodes's monumental history, *The Making of the Atomic Bomb* (New York: Simon and Schuster, 1986), was indispensable both for making the science and technology comprehensible and for its vivid material on all the players, from Vannevar Bush to Enrico Fermi. Another important source was *Reminiscences of Los Alamos, 1943– 1945* (Dordrecht, Holland, and New York: D. Reidel, 1980). Edited by Lawrence Badash, Joseph O. Hirschfelder, and Herbert P. Broida, this useful volume is the fifth in the series *Studies in the History of Modern Science.* The pieces by the late Richard Feynman and George Kistiakowky were especially bright and thoughtful. Women connected to the project often played multiple thankless roles, coping with balky stoves and acting as helpmates to spouses utterly engaged elsewhere. One of our best, most colorful sources was *Standing By and Making Do: Women of Wartime Los Alamos,* edited by Jane S. Wilson and Charlotte Serber (Los Alamos, N. M.: The Los Alamos Historical Society, 1988). This collection of reminiscences by women humanizes the project in ways that no other single source does. We also reread Robert Jungk's classic, *Brighter Than a Thousand Suns: A Personal History of the Atomic Scientists* (San Diego and New York: Harcourt Brace Jovanovich,

1958). Weisskopf's description of how Oppenheimer would seem to materialize just when he was needed is typical of the rich material contained in interviews with the participants conducted by the Los Alamos National Laboratory. Wilson's memory of Oppenheimer is from *All in Our Time,* edited by Jane S. Wilson (New York: Bulletin of the Atomic Scientists, 1974). I. I. Rabi's tribute to Oppie is one of many collected in *Oppenheimer* (New York: Scribners, 1967).

Take-Home Lessons

Released in 1989, the film *Fat Man and Little Boy* was directed by Roland Joffe and written by Bruce Robinson, Tony Garnett, and Joffe. Feynman's tale of how meaning transformed work and his recollection of the aftermath of the Trinity test are both from Badash, et al.

ACKNOWLEDGMENTS

We are enormously grateful to the following people for their help in shaping this book. Charles Handy, James O'Toole, Sam Culbert, Grace Gabe, Kate Bennis, John Bennis, Will Bennis, Nina Steinberg, Eden Steinberg, Charles Carter, and Eric Biederman all read the manuscript at various stages in its evolution and made invaluable suggestions. We benefited greatly from their thoughtful counsel.

We also want to thank our editor at Addison Wesley, John Bell, for his devotion to the project. Our production editor, Beth Burleigh Fuller, was masterful at protecting the book while keeping the schedule, and we are most grateful. Marcy Posner was more than an agent: she counseled us wisely at every turn. Wendy Miller and Irv Biederman were always generous with their encouragement and support. We are also grateful to our indefatigable fact-checker, Kristin Hohenadel; to Marie Christian, for her tireless and intelligent assistance; and to David Simonson, for his thorough research.

Special thanks to the charter students in the "Art and Adventure of Leadership" course at the University of Southern California. They had so much to teach on the subject. Finally, we are grateful to the USC School of Business Administration for its support and encouragement.

INDEX

Index

More Important Lessons from Warren Bennis

On Becoming a Leader
Warren Bennis
"Warren Bennis's most important book"—Peter Drucker
"Crisp and persuasive"—*Fortune*
$14.00, paperback, 0-201-40929-1

Learning to Lead
A Workbook on Becoming a Leader, revised edition
Warren Bennis and Joan Goldsmith
"An excellent vehicle for self-development"
    —Richard Linowes, American University
$15.00, paperback, 0-201-31140-2

An Invented Life
Reflections on Leadership and Change
Warren Bennis
"Like spending several hours in the company of a smart, fascinating man"—*Business Week*
$12.95, paperback, 0-201-62714-0